Pocket Mandarin CHINESE

Dictionary

Compiled by
Philip Yungkin Lee

PERIPLUS

Published by Periplus Editions (HK) Ltd., with editorial offices at
364 Innovation Drive, North Clarendon, Vermont 05759 U.S.A.
and 130 Joo Seng Road #06-01, Singapore 368357.

LCC card No. 2004272611
ISBN-13: 978-0-7946-0043-3
ISBN-10: 0-7946-0043-3

Distributed by:

North America, Latin America & Europe
Tuttle Publishing
364 Innovation Drive
North Clarendon, VT 05759-9436 U.S.A.
Tel: 1 (802) 773-8930   Fax: 1 (802) 773-6993
info@tuttlepublishing.com
www.tuttlepublishing.com

Japan
Tuttle Publishing
Yaekari Building, 3rd Floor
5-4-12 Osaki, Shinagawa-ku
Tokyo 141-0032
Tel: (81) 3 5437-0171   Fax: (81) 3 5437-0755
tuttle-sales@gol.com

Asia-Pacific
Berkeley Books Pte. Ltd.
130 Joo Seng Road #06-01
Singapore 368357
Tel: (65) 6280-1330   Fax: (65) 6280-6290
inquiries@periplus.com.sg
www.periplus.com

10 09 08 07
10 9 8 7 6

Printed in Singapore

C

chá 查 look up (find in book)

chá 茶 tea

chābié 差别 difference
(discrepancy in figures)

cháiyóu 柴油 diesel

cháng 长 long (size)

cháng 尝 to taste, to sample

chángbǐngsháo 长柄勺 ladle,
dipper

chángcháng 常常 often

chángdí 长笛 flute

chángdù 长度 length

chángfāngxíng 长方形
rectangle

chànggē 唱歌 to sing

chángshì 尝试 to attempt

chángtú 长途 long-distance

chángtú diànhuà 长途电话
long-distance call

chángwèi 尝味 to taste
(salty, spicy)

cháo 朝 to, toward (a place)

chāochū 超出 go beyond

chāojí shìchǎng 超级市场
supermarket

chǎojià 吵架 to argue

chāopiào 钞票 note
(currency)

chāoshì 超市 supermarket

cháoshī 潮湿 damp, humid

Cháoxiǎn 朝鲜 North Korea

Cháoxiǎnde 朝鲜的 North
Korean (in general)

Cháoxiǎnyǔ 朝鲜语 Korean
(language)

chāoxiě 抄写 to copy

chātóu 插头 plug (electric)

chāyì 差异 difference (in
quality)

chāzi 叉子 fork

chāzuò 插座 socket (electric)

chē 车 vehicle

chēdào 车道 lane (of a
highway)

chèdǐ 彻底 complete (thorough)

chēfáng 车房 garage (for
parking)

chēkù 车库 garage (for parking)

chēng 称 to weigh

chéng 乘 times (multiplying)

chèng 秤 scales

chéng yīzhíxiàn 成一直线
to line up

chéngběn 成本 cost

chéngchē 乘车 to ride
(transport)

chēngchū 称出 to weigh out

chéngdù 程度 degree, level

chénggōng 成功 success

chénggōng 成功 to succeed

chéngkè 乘客 passenger

chèngpán 称盘 scales

chéngrén 成人 adult

chéngrèn 承认 to admit,
to confess

chéngsè 橙色 orange (color)

chéngshì 城市 city

chéngshí de 诚实的 honest

chéngshìde 城市的 urban

chéngwéi 成为 to become

chéngyuán 成员 member

chénjiù 陈旧 worn out
(clothes, machine)

chénliè 陈列 to display

chénmènde 沉闷的 dull
(weather)

chénmòde 沉默的 silent

chènshān 衬衫 shirt

chényī 晨衣 dressing gown

chī 吃 to eat

chī wǎnfàn 吃晚饭 to eat
dinner

chī wǔfàn 吃午饭 to eat
lunch

chī zǎofàn 吃早饭 to eat
breakfast

chìbǎng 翅膀 wing

chībǎo 吃饱 full, eaten one's
fill

chǐcùn 尺寸 measurements

chídào 迟到 late

chījīng 吃惊 astonished

chīsùde 吃素的 vegetarian

chíxù 持续 last (endure)

chóngbài 崇拜 to worship

chóngfù 重复 to repeat

bìyùn 避孕 contraceptive

bìyùntào 避孕套 condom

bìyùnyào 避孕药 contraceptive pill

bízi 鼻子 nose

bō diànhuà 拨电话 to dial the telephone

bóbo 伯伯 uncle (father's older brother)

bōcài 菠菜 spinach

bófù 伯父 uncle (father's older brother)

bōlàng 波浪 wave (in sea)

bōli 玻璃 glass (material)

bōluó 菠萝 pineapple

bómǔ 伯母 aunt (wife of father's older brother)

bówù 薄雾 mist

bówùguǎn 博物馆 museum

bōyīn 播音 to broadcast

bózi 脖子 neck

bù 不 not

bù 布 cloth

bù 步 step

bù chāochū qínglǐ zhīwài 不超出情理之外 within reason

bù gāoxìng 不高兴 unhappy

bù jígé 不及格 to fail

bù kěnéng 不可能 impossible

bú kèqi 不客气 don't mention it! you're welcome!

bú kèqi de 不客气的 impolite

bú zhèngquè 不正确 wrong (incorrect)

búdàn ... érqiě 不但 ... 而且 not only ... but also

búdàodéde 不道德的 wrong (morally)

bùduì 部队 troops

bùfèn 部分 part (not whole)

búgù 不顾 to ignore

búguì 不贵 reasonable (price)

bùhǎoyìsi 不好意思 embarrassed

bǔhuò 捕获 to capture

bújiànle 不见了 gone, finished

bùjiǔ 不久 soon

bùliào 布料 fabric, textile

bùluò 部落 tribe

bùmén 部门 department

bùrán 不然 else: or else

búshì 不是 no, not (with verbs and adjectives)

bùtóng 不同 difference (in quality)

bùtóngde 不同的 another (different)

búxìng 不幸 misfortune

bùxǔ 不许 to forbid

búyào 不要 don't!

bùzú 不足 lacking

bùzúde 不足的 scarce

C

cāi 猜 to guess

cáichǎn 财产 property

càidān 菜单 menu

cáiliào 材料 material, ingredient

cǎipiào 彩票 lottery

cáiwù 财物 belongings

cāliàng 擦亮 to polish

cān 餐 meal

cángqǐlái 藏起来 to hide

cānguān 参观 to go around, to visit

cāngyíng 苍蝇 fly (insect)

cānjiā 参加 to attend, to join, to go along

cánrěn 残忍 cruel

cānyǔ 参与 to go along, to join in

cǎo 草 grass

cáozáde 嘈杂的 noisy

cáozáshēng 嘈杂声 noise

cāozuò xìtǒng 操作系统 operating system (computer)

cāxǐ 擦洗 to scrub

céng 层 story (building), layer, floor

céng 曾 ever, have already

cèsuǒ 厕所 bathroom, toilet

cèyàn 测验 to test

B

bāokuò 包括 included, including

bǎolěi 堡垒 fortress

bǎoliú 保留 reservation

bǎoliúdì 保留地 reserve (for animals)

bǎomì 保密 to keep a secret

bāopí 剥皮 to peel

bàoqiàn 抱歉 sorry!

bǎowèi 保卫 defend (in war)

bǎoxiǎn 保险 insurance

bàoyuàn 抱怨 to complain

bǎozhèng 保证 guarantee

bāozhuāng 包装 to pack

bāshí 八十 eighty

bǎshǒu 把手 handle

Bāyuè 八月 August

bèi 背 back (part of body)

bèi 被 by (passive voice marker)

bèi jìnzhǐ de 被禁止的 forbidden

bèi shāohuǐ 被烧毁 burned down, out

bèi xiàzhe 被吓着 frightened

bēi'āi 悲哀 sorrow

běibiān 北边 north

Běijīng 北京 Beijing

bèirù 被褥 bedding

bèixīn 背心 vest, undershirt

bēizi 杯子 cup, glass (for drinking)

bèn 笨 stupid

bèng 泵 pump

bēngdài 绷带 bandage

bǐ 比 than

biànhǎo 变好 to get better (improve)

biànhù 辩护 to defend (with words)

biànhuài 变坏 spoiled (of food)

biānjiè 边界 boundary, border

biànlùn 辩论 to argue

biànmì 便秘 constipation

biàntiáo 便条 note (written)

biànwèide 变味的 spoiled (of food)

biānyuán 边缘 border, edge

biānzào 编造 make up, invent

biānzhì 编制 to weave

biǎo 表 watch (wristwatch)

biǎogé 表格 form (to fill out)

biǎomiàn 表面 surface

biǎoshì 表示 to express, to state

biǎoshì bùmǎn 表示不满 to frown (express dissatisfaction)

biāotí 标题 title (of book, film)

biǎoxiàn 表现 behave

biǎoyǎn 表演 show (live performance)

biǎoyáng 表扬 to praise

biāozhì 标记 sign, symbol

biāozhǔn 标准 level (standard)

bié zài zhèyàng 别再这样 stop it!

biéde 别的 anything else, other

bǐjiào 比较 to compare, rather, fairly

bǐjiào hǎo 比较好 better

bǐjìběn 笔记本 notebook

bíkǒng 鼻孔 nostril

bīn'guǎn 宾馆 guesthouse, hotel

bīng 冰 ice

bìng 病 illness

bīngdòng 冰冻 frozen

bǐnggān 饼干 biscuit

bīngjīlíng 冰激凌 ice cream

bìngle 病了 sick, ill

bīngqílín 冰淇淋 ice cream

bìngrén 病人 patient (doctor's)

bīngxiāng 冰箱 refrigerator

bīngzhèn 冰镇 chilled

bǐrú 比如 for example

bǐsài 比赛 match, game, competition

bìxū 必须 must, to need

bìxū 必需 necessary

bǐyì 笔译 to translate

Chinese–English

A

ǎi 矮 short (not tall)

ài 爱 to love

Ài'ěrlán 爱尔兰 Ireland

Ài'ěrlánde 爱尔兰的 Irish (in general)

Ài'ěrlánrén 爱尔兰人 Irish (people)

àihào 爱好 hobby

àihù 爱护 care for, love

àiqíng 爱情 love

àizībìng 艾滋病 AIDS

àn 暗 dark

ángguì 昂贵 costly

ānjìng 安静 quiet

ànlíng 按铃 to ring a bell

ànmó 按摩 to massage

ānpái 安排 to organize, to arrange; arrangements, planning

ānquán 安全 secure, safe

Àodàlìyà 澳大利亚 Australia

Àodàlìyàde 澳大利亚的 Australian (in general)

Àodàlìyàrén 澳大利亚人 Australian (people)

Àolínpǐkè Yùndònghuì 奥林匹克运动会 Olympics

Àomén 澳门 Macau

Àoyùnhuì 奥运会 Olympics

Àozhōu 澳洲 Australia

Àozhōude 澳洲的 Australian (in general)

Àozhōurén 澳洲人 Australian (people)

āsīpǐlín 阿司匹林 aspirin

B

... ba ... 吧 let's (suggestion)

bā 八 eight

bǎ 把 with regard to (object marker)

bǎ ... jiāo gěi 把 ... 交给 leave behind for safekeeping

bàba 爸爸 father

bàgōng 罢工 to go on strike

bǎi 百 hundred

bái jiàngyóu 白酱油 soy sauce (salty)

bǎi zhuōzi 摆桌子 lay the table

báicài 白菜 cabbage, Chinese

bǎifēnbǐ 百分比 percentage

bǎifēnzhī ... 百分之 ... percent

bǎihuò shāngdiàn 百货商店 department store

báisè 白色 white

báitiān 白天 daytime

bǎituō 摆脱 rid: get rid of

bǎiwàn 百万 million

bān 搬 to move from one place to another

bàn 半 half

bàn 瓣 cloves

bàn'gōngshì 办公室 office

bāngmáng 帮忙 to help

bāngzhu 帮助 to assist, assistance

bānjī 班机 flight

bānjiā 搬家 to move house

bānjīhào 班机号 flight number

bànlǚ 伴侣 partner (spouse)

bànshúde 半熟的 rare (uncooked)

bāo 包 to pack, to wrap

bào 报 newspaper

bàogào 报告 report

bàoguān 报关 declare (customs)

bāoguǒ 包裹 package, parcel

bǎohù 保护 to guard

Tones

A tone is a variation in pitch by which a syllable can be pronounced. In Chinese, a variation of pitch or tone changes the meaning of the word. There are four tones each marked by a diacritic. In addition there is a neutral tone which does not carry any tone marks. Below is a tone chart which describes tones using the 5-degree notation. It divides the range of pitches from lowest (1) to highest (5). Note that the neutral tone is not shown on the chart as it is affected by the tone that precedes it.

Tone chart

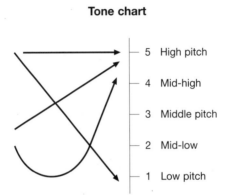

— 5	High pitch
— 4	Mid-high
— 3	Middle pitch
— 2	Mid-low
— 1	Low pitch

The first tone is a high-level tone represented by a level tone mark (–). The second tone is a high-rising tone represented by a rising tone mark (ˊ). The third tone is a low-dipping tone represented by a dish-like tone mark (ˇ). The fourth tone is a high-falling tone represented by an falling tone mark (ˋ). The neutral tone is pronounced light and soft in comparison to other tones and is not marked by any tone mark. A syllable is said to take on a neutral tone when it forms part of a word or is placed in various parts of a sentence.

Pronunciation

The imitated pronunciation should be read as if it were English, bearing in mind the following main points:

Consonants

b, **d**, **f**, **g**, **h**, **k**, **l**, **m**, **n**, **p**, **s**, **t**, **w**, **y** as in English

c   like English **ts** in i**ts**

j   like English **j** in **j**ee

q   like English **ch** in **ch**eer, with a strong puff of air

r   like English **ur** in leis**ur**e, with the tongue rolled back

x   like English **see** (whole word)

z   like English **ds** in ki**ds**

ch like English **ch** in **ch**ur**ch**, with the tongue rolled back and a strong puff of air

sh like English **sh** in **sh**e, with the tongue rolled back

zh like English **j**, with the tongue rolled back

Vowels

a   like English **ar** in f**ar**

e   like English **er** in h**er**

i   like English **ee** in f**ee**

o   like English **or** in f**or**

u   like English **ue** in s**ue**

ü   like French **u**

geographically separated regions who would not be able to understand each other's everyday speech.

The characters derived initially from the stylized representation of concrete objects, to which the abstract meanings needed for the expression of the whole language have been added by processes of combination and metaphor. The earliest written records of Chinese date back to the second millennium BCE, in the form of marks scratched on bones and shells used in a system of divination. The shapes of these characters are very different from the modern forms, but the development of the script from a directly representational system is already well advanced.

Classical Chinese literature dates from around 1500 BCE, and there has been some development of the characters over the succeeding centuries. Since the 1950s the government of the PRC has promoted the simplification of a number of characters that are complex in formation or contain a large number of strokes, and the reform has also been adopted in Singapore. All the Chinese words and phrases in this dictionary are written in these simplified characters. In Taiwan and Hong Kong the traditional forms of the characters are mostly still used, but the simplified forms are also readily understood.

In this dictionary every Chinese word and phrase is also given in the roman alphabet, following the official system of transcription promulgated in 1958 and known as *Hanyu Pinyin*. A guide to the pronunciation of the romanized forms is given on the following pages.

Chinese is a tonal language, and it is extremely important to use the correct tone in pronouncing each syllable. In this dictionary the tones are indicated by diacritical marks over the vowels.

The words and phrases in the Chinese–English section of the dictionary are arranged in English alphabetical order using the letters and diacritical marks of the Hanyu Pinyin system of romanization. Words that have the same spelling but different tones are listed in order of their tones: first, second, third, fourth and neutral tone. For example, 'ǎi short' comes before 'ài to love'. Words that have the same spelling and the same tone are listed according to the complexity of the Chinese characters. For example, 'gān dry' with three strokes comes before 'gān liver' with seven strokes.

Although the writing system and pronunciation of Chinese may be daunting for English speakers, grammatically it is not too problematic. There are no inflections as such (distinctions such as tense and number being indicated by various particles) and the word order is generally the same as in English.

Introduction

This Pocket Dictionary is an indispensable companion for visitors to China and for anyone in the early stages of learning Chinese. It contains all the 3,000 or so Chinese words that are most commonly encountered in colloquial, everyday speech.

For the sake of clarity, only the common Chinese equivalents for each English word have been given. When an English word has more than one possible meaning, with different Chinese equivalents, each meaning is listed separately, with a clear explanatory gloss. The layout is clear and accessible, with none of the abbreviations and dense nests of entries typical of many small dictionaries.

The language represented in this dictionary is Modern Standard Chinese, which is also commonly known in English as Mandarin, and in China as *Putonghua* (literally 'Modern Standard Chinese') and Taiwan as *Guoyu* (literally 'national speech').

The People's Republic of China has a population of over 1.35 billion people, more than 90% of whom are ethnically Chinese. They speak a large number of related languages, often collectively referred to as 'Chinese dialects'. Many of these are mutually unintelligible in their spoken forms, although they are united by a common system of writing (see further below).

The main language groups are Mandarin, spoken in a broad area across the north and west of the country, Kan, Xiang, Wu, Northern Min, Southern Min, Hakka, and Cantonese. Most of these also contain within them a wide range of dialectal variation, especially as regards pronunciation and elements of vocabulary.

Modern Standard Chinese is based on the northern Mandarin dialects of the area surrounding the capital Beijing, and the standard pronunciation is that traditionally used in Beijing. Its use has been widely promoted as an instrument of national unity since the overthrow of the Manchu monarchy by the native Han Chinese in 1912, and especially since the founding of the PRC in 1949. Nowadays most people in China have a good knowledge of it even if they do not commonly speak it in daily life.

The written form of Chinese does not relate directly to the sounds of the language. Instead it makes use of a very large number of characters representing different syllables, to each of which is linked both a meaning and a sound. The meaning attached to each character is the same for each of the Chinese languages and dialects, although the way it is pronounced may well be different. In this way writing can serve as a means of communication between Chinese from

Contents

C

chǒnghuàide 宠坏的 spoiled (of children)

chōnglàng 冲浪 surf

chǒngwù 宠物 pet animal

chōngxǐ 冲洗 to develop film

chóngzi 虫子 insect

chǒu 丑 ugly

chóubàn 筹办 to arrange

chóuhèn 仇恨 hatred

chòuqì 臭气 odor, bad smell

chōutī 抽屉 drawer

chòuwèi 臭味 smell, bad odor

chōuyān 抽烟 smoke, to (tobacco)

chù 触 to touch

chú yú 除于 divided by

chū zhǔyi 出主意 to advise

chuān 穿 to put on (clothes)

chuán 船 boat, ship

chuānbàn 穿扮 to get dressed

chuáng 床 bed

chuángdān 床单 bedsheet

chuángdiàn 床垫 mattress

chuānghu 窗户 window (in house)

chuāngkǒu 窗口 window (for paying, buying tickets)

chuānglián 窗帘 curtain

chuàngzào 创造 to create

chuàngzuò 创作 to create

chuánrǎn de 传染的 contagious

chuànròuqiān 串肉扦 skewer

chuánshuō 传说 legend

chuántǒngde 传统的 traditional

chuánxùn 传讯 to call, to summon

chuánzhēn 传真 fax (message)

chuánzhēnjī 传真机 fax (machine)

chūbǎn 出版 to publish

chūchù 出处 source

chūfā 出发 departure

chùfàn 触犯 to offend

chúfáng 厨房 kitchen

chúfēi 除非 unless

chūhàn 出汗 to perspire

chuízhíde 垂直的 vertical

chūkǒu 出口 to export, export, exit

chúle ... yǐwài 除了 ... 以外 apart from, besides, except

chùlǐ 处理 to handle, to manage

chūlù 出路 way out

chūmíng 出名 famous

chǔn 蠢 stupid

chúnde 纯的 pure

chūntiān 春天 spring (season)

chūqù 出去 go out, exit

chūqù zǒuzou 出去走走 go for a walk

chūshēng 出生 to be born

chūshēng rìqī 出生日期 date of birth

chúshī 厨师 cook (person)

chūshòu 出售 for sale

chūxiàn 出现 appear, become visible

chǔzáng 储藏 to store

chūzūqìchē 出租汽车 taxi

cí 词 word

cìchuān 刺穿 pierce, penetrate

cíde 雌的 female

cídiǎn 词典 dictionary

cípán 磁盘 diskette (computer)

cǐwài 此外 in addition

cìxiù 刺绣 embroidery

cìxù 次序 sequence, order

cìyào de 次要的 minor (not important)

cóng 从 from

cóng ... yàngzi kànlái 从 ... 样子看来 by way of

cónglái méiyǒu 从来没有 never

cónglín 丛林 jungle

cōngmíng 聪明 clever, smart, wise

cù 醋 vinegar

cuīcù 催促 to urge, to push for

cuīhuǐ 摧毁 destroyed, ruined

cūlǔde 粗鲁的 rough (not gentle)

C

cūlüède 粗略地 roughly, approximately
cún 存 save, keep
cúnfàng 存放 deposit (leave behind with someone)
cúnkuǎn 存款 deposit (put money in the bank)
cúnxīn 存心 intention
cúnzài 存在 to exist
cūnzhuāng 村庄 village
cuòde 错的 wrong (mistaken)
cuòwù 错误 error, mistake

D

... de shíhou ... 的时候 when, at the time
dǎ 打 to hit, to strike
dà 大 big, large
dà bùfèn 大部分 mostly
dǎ diànhuà 打电话 call on the telephone
dǎ fángyìzhēn 打防疫针 vaccination
dǎ hēqiàn 打呵欠 to yawn
dà jiànmài 大贱买 sale (reduced prices)
dǎ pēntì 打喷嚏 to sneeze
dà shuǐguàn 大水罐 pitcher, jug
dǎ zhāohu 打招呼 greetings
dǎbài 打败 to defeat
dǎbàn 打扮 to get dressed
dàbiàn 大便 to defecate
dàbó 大伯 brother-in-law (husband's older brother)
dádào 达到 to attain, to reach
dǎfān 打翻 overturned
dáfù 答复 to reply, response
dàgài 大概 about (approximately), probably
dǎhuǒjī 打火机 lighter
dài 带 to carry
dài wènhǎo 代问好 to say hello
dàifu 大夫 doctor

dàitì 代替 to replace, instead of
dàizi 袋子 bag
dǎjī 打击 to strike, to hit
dǎjià 打架 to fight (physically)
dǎjiǎo 打搅 to bother, to disturb
dàjīngxiǎoguàide 大惊小怪的 fussy
dǎkāi 打开 to open
dǎléi 打雷 thunder
dàlóu 大楼 building
dàlù 大陆 continent
dàmén 大门 gate (main entrance)
dàmǐ 大米 rice (uncooked grains)
dàn'gāo 蛋糕 cake, pastry
dān'ge 耽搁 to delay
dānbǎo 担保 to guarantee
dānchéngpiào 单程票 one-way ticket
dānchúnde 单纯的 plain (not fancy)
dāndiào 单调 bland
dāndú 单独 alone
dāngjīn 当今 nowadays
dāngrán 当然 of course
dāngrán kěyǐ 当然可以 certainly!
dāngzhōng 当中 be in the middle of doing
dānshēn 单身 single (not married)
dànshì 但是 but, however
dānxīn 担心 to worry
dānyī 单一 single (only one)
dǎo 岛 island
dào 到 to arrive
dào 倒 to pour
dào ... li 到 ... 里 into
dàobié 道别 to say goodbye
dàochù 到处 everywhere
dàodá 到达 arrival
dāodòu 刀豆 kidney beans
Dàojiào 道教 Taoism
dǎoméi 倒霉 bad luck
dǎoméide 倒霉的 unlucky
dàoqiàn 道歉 to apologize

dàotián 稻田 rice fields

dǎotuì 倒退 to reverse, to back up

dǎoxiàlái 倒下来 to fall over

dàoxiè 道谢 to say thank you

dǎoyóu 导游 to guide someone somewhere

dǎozhuàn 倒转 upside down

dāozi 刀子 knife

dàozi 稻子 rice (plant)

dǎpòle 打破了 broken, shattered

dǎrǎo 打扰 to bother, disturb

dàshēng 大声 loud

dàshǐ 大使 ambassador

dàshǐguǎn 大使馆 embassy

dàsuàn 大蒜 garlic

dǎsuàn 打算 to intend, to plan

dǎsuàn ... yòng de 打算 ...用的 intended for

dàtóuzhēn 大头针 pin

dàtuǐ 大腿 thigh

dàxiàng 大象 elephant

dàxiǎo 大小 size

dàxué 大学 university

dàyī 大衣 coat, overcoat

dǎyìn 打印 to print (computer)

dāyìng 答应 to promise

dàyuē 大约 around (approximately)

dǎzhàng 打仗 to make war

dǎzhēn 打针 injection

dǎzì 打字 to type

dédào 得到 to get, to receive

Déguó 德国 Germany

Déguóde 德国的 German (in general)

Déguórén 德国人 German (people)

děi 得, have to, must

dēng 灯 light (lamp)

děng 等 to wait for

děng yīxià 等一下 in a moment, just a moment

dēngshàng 登上 to go up, to climb

dèngzi 凳子 stool

Déwén 德文 German (language)

Déyǔ 德语 German (language)

dézuì 得罪 offend

dī 低 low

dǐ 底 bottom (base)

dì 地 land

dì'èr 第二 second (in sequence)

diàn 电 electric

diǎn(zhōng) 点(钟) o'clock

diǎncài 点菜 to order (food)

diāndǎo 颠倒 upside down

diàndòng lóutī 电动楼梯 escalator

diànfēngshàn 电风扇 fan (electrical)

diànhuà 电话 telephone

diànhuà hàomǎ 电话号码 telephone number

diànhuà liúyán 电话留言 voicemail

diǎnlǐ 典礼 ceremony

diànliú 电流 electricity

diànnǎo 电脑 computer

diànqì 电器 electrical appliance

diànshì 电视 television

diànshìjī 电视机 TV set

diàntī 电梯 lift, elevator

diǎnxíngde 典型的 typical

diànyǐng 电影 film, movie

diànyǐngyuàn 电影院 cinema

diànzhǔ 店主 shopkeeper

diànzi 电子 electronic

diànzi 垫子 tablemat

diànzi yóujiàn 电子邮件 email (message)

diāo 雕 to engrave

diàochá 调查 to research

diāokèpǐn 雕刻品 carving

diāosù 雕塑 sculpture, to sculpt

diàoxià 掉下 to fall

diāoxiàng 雕像 statue

diàoyú 钓鱼 to fish

dìdi 弟弟 brother (younger)

dìfang 地方 place, space

D

dìmèi 弟妹 sister-in-law (wife of husband's younger brother)

dìmiàn 地面 ground, earth

dǐng 顶 top

dǐngduān 顶端 end (tip)

dǐngfēng 顶峰 peak, summit

dìnggòu 订购 / 定购 order (placed for goods)

dìnghūn 订婚 / 定婚 engaged (to be married)

dìngqī 定期 regular, normal

dīngzi 钉子 nail (spike)

dìqiú 地球 Earth, the world

dìqū 地区 area, region

díquè 的确 quite (very)

dírén 敌人 enemy

dìsān 第三 third (in a series)

dìtǎn 地毯 carpet

dìtú 地图 map

diūshī 丢失 to lose, to mislay

diūxià 丢下 to leave behind by accident

dìwèi 地位 rank, station in life

dìwèi gāo de 地位高的 ranking

dìxí 地席 mat

dìxí 弟媳 sister-in-law (wife of husband's younger brother)

dìzhèn 地震 earthquake

dìzhǐ 地址 address

dǒng 懂 understand

dòng 洞 hole

dōngběi 东北 north-east

dōngbiān 东边 east

dōngnán 东南 south-east

dǒngshìzhǎng 董事长 director (of company)

dōngtiān 冬天 winter

dòngwù 动物 animal

dòngwùyuán 动物园 zoo

dōngxi 东西 object, thing

dòngzuò 动作 movement, motion

dōu 都 all

dòu 豆 bean

dòuchǐ 豆豉 black beans

dòufu 豆腐 tofu, beancurd

dù 度 degrees (temperature)

duǎn 短 short (concise)

duànkāi 断开 broken off

duǎnkù 短裤 shorts (short trousers)

duǎnnèikù 短内裤 shorts (underpants)

duǎnzàn 短暂 short time, a moment

duǎnzànde 短暂的 brief

dǔbó 赌博 gamble

dùchuán 渡船 ferry

duì 队 team

duì 对 correct/toward (a person)

duì ... zhòu méitou 对 ... 皱眉头 to frown

duìbuqǐ 对不起 sorry!

duìdài 对待 to treat (behave towards)

duìfù 对付 make do

duìhuàn 兑换 change, exchange (money)

duìhuànlǜ 兑换率 exchange rate

duìjiǎode 对角地 diagonally

duìjiǎoxiàn 对角线 diagonal

duìlìde 对立的 opposed, in opposition

duìmiàn 对面 opposite (facing)

duìshǒu 对手 rival, opponent

duìxiàn 兑现 to cash a check

dùjì 妒忌 to be jealous

dúlìde 独立的 own, on one's

duō 多 much, many

Duō cháng? 多长? how long?

Duō dà suìshù? 多大岁数? how old?

Duō dà niánjì? 多大年纪? how old?

duō yīdiǎnr 多一点儿 more (comparative)

Duō yuǎn? 多远? how far?

Duōshao qián? 多少钱? how much?

duōyúde 多余的 unnecessary

duōyún 多云 cloudy, overcast

dúpǐn 毒品 drug (recreational)

dúyào 毒药 poison

dùzi 肚子 stomach, belly

E

é 蛾 moth

é 鹅 goose

é 额 forehead

è 饿 hungry

èr 二 two (numeral)

ěrduo 耳朵 ear

ěrhuán 耳环 earrings

érqiě 而且 moreover

èrshí 二十 twenty

Èryuè 二月 February

érzi 儿子 son

éwàide 额外的 extra

F

fā báirìmèng 发白日梦 to daydream

fā chuánzhēn 发传真 to fax

fā diànzi yóujiàn 发电子邮件 to email

fā yīmèir 发依妹儿 to email

fāchòu 发臭 to stink

fādòng 发动 to start

fādòngjī 发动机 engine

fādǒu 发抖 to shiver

Fǎguó 法国 France

Fǎguóde 法国的 French (in general)

Fǎguórén 法国人 French (people)

fákuǎn 罚款 fine (punishment)

fāliàng 发亮 shiny

fǎlǜ 法律 laws, legislation

fāmíng 发明 to invent

fān'guòlái 翻过来 over: to turn over

fàncài 饭菜 dish (particular food)

fāndǎo 翻倒 to turn over

fǎnduì 反对 to object, to protest

fàng 放 to put, to place

fāngbiàn 方便 convenient

fāngfǎ 方法 way, method

fānggéde 方格的 checked (pattern)

fángjiān 房间 room (in hotel)

fàngqíngle 放晴了 clear (of weather)

fángshàiyóu 防晒油 sunscreen lotion

fàngsōng 放松 to relax

fànguǎn 饭馆 restaurant

fǎngwèn 访问 to pay a visit

fāngxiàng 方向 direction

fāngxíngde 方形的 square (shape)

fāngyán 方言 dialect

fǎngzàode 仿造的 patterned

fángzi 房子 house

fánmèn 烦闷 upset, unhappy

fánnǎode 烦恼的 troublesome

fánrǎo 烦扰 bother, disturbance

fànwéi 范围 area

fǎnxiàngde 反响的 reversed, backwards

fānyì 翻译 to translate, translator, interpreter

fǎnyìng 反应 to react, reaction, response

fǎnyìng 反映 to reflect

fāpiào 发票 invoice

fāshāo 发烧 fever

fāshēng 发生 happen, occur

fāshēng shénme shì 发生什么事 what happened?

Fǎwén 法文 French (language)

fāxiàn 发现 to discover

fāyīn 发音 to pronounce

Fǎyǔ 法语 French (language)

fāzhǎn 发展 development

fēi 飞 to fly

fèi 肺 lungs

fēicháng 非常 really (very)

fēifǎ 非法 illegal

F

fèihuà 废话 nonsense
fēijī 飞机 aeroplane, airplane
fēijīchǎng 飞机场 airport
Fēilùbīn 菲律宾 Philippines
Fēilùbīnde 菲律宾的 Filipino
(in general)
Fēilùbīnrén 菲律宾人 Filipino
(people)
Fēilùbīnyǔ 菲律宾语 Filipino
(language)
fēiqiángzhìde 非强制的
optional
féiwòde 肥沃的 fertile
fèiyòng 费用 cost (expense)
féizào 肥皂 soap
fēn(zhōng) 分(钟) minute
fēnfā 分发 hand out
fēng 风 wind, breeze
féng 缝 to sew
fēngbào 风暴 storm
fēnggé 风格 style
fēngjǐng 风景 view,
panorama
fēngkuángde 疯狂的 insane,
crazy
fēngmì 蜂蜜 honey
fēngsuǒ 封锁 closed (road)
fēngwèi fàncài 风味饭菜
cooking, cuisine
fēnháng 分行 branch
fēnhóngsè 粉红色 pink
fēnjī 分机 extension
(telephone)
fēnkāi 分开 to divide, split up
fēnkāile 分开了 broken off
fēnlíde 分离的 separate
fénmù 坟墓 grave
fènnù 愤怒 anger
Fójiào 佛教 Buddhism
Fójiàode 佛教的 Buddhist
(in general)
Fójiàotú 佛教徒 Buddhist
(people)
fǒuzé 否则 else: or else
fǔbài 腐败 corrupt
fùběn 副本 copy
fùbù 腹部 abdomen
fúcóng 服从 to obey

fúcóngde 服从的 obedient
fùdāndeqǐ 负担得起
to afford
fúhé biāozhǔn 符合标准
measure up to standard
fùjìn 附近 nearby
fǔlànde 腐烂的 rotten
fùmǔ 父母 parents
fùqián 付钱 to pay
fùqin 父亲 father
fūren 夫人 madam
(term of address)
fúshǒuyǐ 扶手椅 armchair
fúwù 服务 service
fúwùyuán 服务员 waiter,
waitress
fùxìn 复信 to reply
(in writing)
fǔyǎng 抚养 to raise
(children)
fùyìn 复印 to photocopy,
photocopy
fùyìnjiàn 复印件 photocopy
fùyǒude 富有的 wealthy
fùyù 富裕 well off, wealthy
fùyùde 富裕的 rich
fùzá 复杂 complicated
fùzé 负责 to take care of,
to be responsible
fúzhuāng 服装 costume

G

gài 盖 to build, to cover
gǎibiàn 改变 to change
(conditions, situations)
gǎibiàn zhǔyi 改变主意
to change one's mind
gàizhāng 盖章 stamp (ink)
gǎizhèng 改正 to correct
gàizi 盖子 lid
gān 干 dry
gān 肝 liver
gàn 干 do
gǎn xìngqù 感兴趣
interested in
gānbēi 干杯 cheers!

gǎnchū 赶出 chase away, chase out

gǎndào jīngyà 感到惊讶 astonished

gǎndào xīngfèn 感到兴奋 excited

gǎndào yíhàn 感到遗憾 to regret

gāngbǐ 钢笔 pen

gāngcái 刚才 just now

gǎngkǒu 港口 harbor

gāngmén 肛门 anus

gāngtiě 钢铁 steel

gǎnjī 感激 grateful

gānjìng 干净 clean

gǎnjué 感觉 feeling

gānjúshǔde 柑橘属的 citrus

gǎnkuài! 赶快 hurry up!

gǎnmào 感冒 cold, flu

gǎnqíng 感情 emotion

gǎnxiè 感谢 to thank

gānzào 干燥 dry (weather)

gānzhè 甘蔗 sugarcane

gāo 高 high, tall

gāo'ěrfūqiú 高尔夫球 golf

gāodù 高度 level (height)

Gāomián 高棉 Cambodia

Gāomiánde 高棉的 Cambodian (in general)

Gāomiánrén 高棉人 Cambodian (people)

Gāomiányǔ 高棉语 Cambodian (language)

gàosu 告诉 to let someone know

gāowán 睾丸 testicles

gāoxìng 高兴 glad, pleased, happy

gāoyǎ 高雅 elegant

gē 割 to cut

gē 歌 song

gèshì-gèyàng 各式各样 every kind of

gèbié 个别 different, other

gēbo 胳膊 arm

gēge 哥哥 brother (older)

gěi 给 to give

gěi ... kàn 给 ... 看 to show

gěi rén shēnkè yìnxiàng 给人深刻印象 to make an impression

gěi rén shēnkè yìnxiàng de 给人深刻印象的 impressive

gēn 根 root (of plant)

gēn 跟 ... with

gēn ... bǐjiào 跟 ... 比较 compared with

gēn ... liánxì 跟 ... 联系 to contact, get in touch with

gēn shāngliang 跟 ...商量 to consult, talk over with

gènghǎo 更好 better

gèngduōde 更多的 more of (things)

gènghuàile 更坏了 worse

gèngshǎode 更少的 less (smaller amount)

gēnjù 根据 based on, according to

gēnsuí 跟随 following

gēnzhe 跟着 to follow behind

gōng'ānjú 公安局 police

gōngchǎng 工厂 factory

gōngchǐ 公尺 meter

gōngdào 公道 reasonable (price)

gōngdiàn 宫殿 palace

gōnggòng 公共 public

gōnggòngqìchē 公共汽车 bus

gōngjī 攻击 attack (in war)

gōngjiàng 工匠 craftsperson

gōngjīn 公斤 kilogram

gōngjù 工具 tool

gōnglǐ 公里 kilometer

gōngmín 公民 citizen

gōngpíng 公平 just, fair

gōngsī 公司 company, firm

gōngwénbāo 公文包 briefcase

gōngyù 公寓 apartment, flat

gōngyuán 公园 garden, park

gōngzī 工资 wages, salary

gōngzuò 工作 job, work

gōngzuò rényuán 工作人员 staff

G

gōngzuòrì 工作日 day of the week

gǒu 狗 dog

gòuwù 购物 shop, go shopping

gǔ shíhou 古时候 olden times, in

guā 瓜 melon

guà 挂 to hang

guā húzi 刮胡子 to shave

guǎfù 寡妇 widow

guàhào 挂号 to register

guàhàoxìn 挂号信 registered post

guān'guāng 观光 sightseeing

guānbì 关闭 shut

guānfū 鳏夫 widower

guǎngbō 广播 broadcast

guǎngchǎng 广场 square, town square

guāngdié 光碟 CD

guǎngkuòde 广阔的 broad, spacious

guāngpán 光盘 CD

guāngpán yuèdúqì 光盘阅读器 CD-ROM

guāngtūde 光秃的 bald

Guǎngzhōu 广州 Guangzhou (Canton)

Guǎngzhōuhuà 广州话 Cantonese

guànjūn 冠军 champion

guānkàn 观看 to view, to look at, to watch

guānle 关了 off (turned off)

guǎnlǐ 管理 manage, succeed

guānmén 关门 closed (door/shop)

guānshàngle 关上了 closed

guānshuì 关税 duty (import tax)

guàntóu 罐头 can, tin

guānxìwǎng 关系网 network

guānyú 关于 concerning

guānyuán 官员 officials (government)

gǔdài 古代 ancient

gùdìngde 固定的 regular, normal

gūdú 孤独 lonely

gūgu 姑姑 aunt (father's younger sister)

guǐ 鬼 ghost

guì 贵 costly, expensive

guìbīn 贵宾 guest of honor

guīdìngde 规定的 compulsory

guīhuán 归还 to return, to give back

guījiù 归咎 to blame

guījù 规矩 rules

guījùde 规矩的 well-behaved

guìtái 柜台 counter (for paying, buying tickets)

guìzi 柜子 cupboard

gǔjì 古迹 remains (historical)

gūmǔ 姑母 aunt (father's older sister)

gùn 棍 stick, pole

gūniang 姑娘 girl

guō 锅 pan

guò 过 cross, go over

guò yīhuǐr 过一会儿 later

guòcuò 过错 fault

guòde kuàihuó 过得快活 to enjoy oneself

guòfèn 过分 too much

guójí 国籍 nationality

guójì 国际 international

guójì xiàngqí 国际象棋 chess

guójiā 国家 country (nation)

guǒjiàng 果酱 jam

guòqùde 过去的 past, former

guówài 国外 abroad

guówáng 国王 king

guòyè 过夜 to stay overnight

Guóyǔ 国语 Mandarin (language) (Taiwan and Hong Kong)

guǒzhī 果汁 juice

gùshi 故事 story (tale)

gùtǐde 固体的 solid

gǔtou 骨头 bone

gǔwán 古玩 antiques

gūzhàng 姑丈 uncle (husband of father's sister)

H

hǎi 海 sea
hái méiyǒu 还没有 yet: not yet
hǎi/lù yóujì 海 / 陆邮寄
    surface mail
hǎigǎng 海港 port
háiguī 海龟 turtle (sea)
hǎimián 海绵 sponge
hàipà 害怕 scared
hǎitān 海滩 beach
hǎiwài 海外 abroad
hǎiwān 海湾 bay
hǎixiá 海峡 strait
hǎixiān 海鲜 seafood
hǎiyáng 海洋 ocean
háizi 孩子 child (offspring)
hǎn 喊 to cry out
hàn 汗 sweat
hángkōng yóujiàn 航空邮件
    airmail
Hánguó 韩国 South Korea
Hánguóde 韩国的 South
    Korean (in general)
Hánguórén 韩国人 South
    Korean (people)
hángxíng 航行 to sail
hánhúde 含糊的 vague
hànkù 汗裤 shorts (underpants)
hánqiān qìyóu 含铅汽油
    leaded petrol
hànshān 汗衫 teeshirt
Hánwén 韩文 Korean
    (language)
Hányǔ 韩语 Korean (language)
Hànyǔ 汉语 Chinese (language)
hànzāi 旱灾 drought
Hànzì 汉字 character (Chinese)
háo 蚝 oyster
hǎo 好 well (good), nice, fine
    (okay)
hǎochī 好吃 delicious, tasty
háohuáde 豪华的 luxurious
hǎojíle 好极了 wonderful
hǎokàn 好看 beautiful (of
    things)
hàomǎ 号码 number
háomǐ 毫米 millimeter

hǎowánr 好玩儿 fun
hǎoxiàng 好象 to resemble
hǎoxiào 好笑 funny
hǎozhuǎn 好转 to get better
hàozi 耗子 rat
hē 喝 to drink
hé 河 river
hé 和 and
hé'àn 河岸 bank (of river)
héchéngde 合成的 synthetic
héfǎ 合法 legal
héhuǒrén 合伙人 partner
    (in business)
hēi hújiāo 黑胡椒 pepper
    (black)
hēi jiàngyóu 黑酱油 soy sauce
    (sweet)
hēi'àn 黑暗 dark
hēisè 黑色 black
hélándòu 荷兰豆 snowpeas
hěn 很 very, extremely
hèn 恨 to hate
hěnduō 很多 a lot, many, much
héngguò 横过 across
hěnkuàide 很快的 quickly
hěnshǎo 很少 seldom
hépíng 和平 peace
hépíngde 和平的 peaceful
héqǐ 合起 to close, to cover
héqínglǐde 合情理的 sensible
hèsè 褐色 brown
héshí 何时 when
héshì cídài 盒式磁带 cassette
héshìde 合适的 suitable,
    fitting, compatible
hésuàn 核算 count, calculate
hétóng 合同 contract
hézi 盒子 box (cardboard)
hēzuì 喝醉 to be drunk
hóng pútaojiǔ 红葡萄酒 red
    wine
hōngkǎo 烘烤 roasted, grilled,
    toasted
hóngsè 红色 red
hóngshuǐ 洪水 flood
hòu 厚 thick (of things)
hòuhuǐ 后悔 sorry, to feel
    regretful

H

hòulái 后来 afterwards, then

hóulóng 喉咙 throat

hòumiàn 后面 back, rear, tail

hòutiān 后天 day after tomorrow

hòuyì 后裔 descendant

hóuzi 猴子 monkey

hú 壶 jug, pot

hú 湖 lake

huā 花 flower

huà 画 to draw

huācài 花菜 cauliflower

huàhuàr 画画儿 paint a picture

huái 踝 ankle

huài 坏 bad

huàile 坏了 broken, does not work, off (gone bad)

huáiyí 怀疑 to suspect

huáiyùn 怀孕 pregnant

huàn 换 change, switch (clothes)

huángguā 黄瓜 cucumber

huánghūn 黄昏 dusk

huángsè 黄色 yellow

huángyóu 黄油 butter

huánjìng 环境 surroundings, environment

huánrào 环绕 round, around

huānyíng 欢迎 to greet, to welcome, welcome!

huāpíng 花瓶 vase

huāqián 花钱 to spend (money)

huàr 画儿 painting

huāshēngmǐ 花生米 peanut

huāyuán 花园 garden, yard

huàzhuāngpǐn 化妆品 cosmetics

húdié 蝴蝶 butterfly

hūhǎn 呼喊 to shout

huìbào 汇报 to report

huīchén 灰尘 dust

huídá 回答 to answer, to respond (spoken)

huīfú 恢复 recover, resume

huìhuà 会话 conversation

huìhuà 绘画 painting

huíjiā 回家 to go home

huílái 回来 to come back

huíqù 回去 to return, to go back

huīsè 灰色 gray

huítóu jiàn 回头见 see you later!

huíyì 回忆 memories

huìyì 会议 meeting

húluóbo 胡萝卜 carrot

hùnhé 混合 to mix

hùnhéde 混合的 mixed

hūnlǐ 婚礼 wedding

hùnluàn 混乱 confused (in a mess)

hùnxiáo 混淆 to confuse

huǒ 火 fire

huò duō huò shǎo 或多或少 more or less

huǒbàn 伙伴 partner (spouse)

huǒchái 火柴 matches

huǒchē 火车 train

huǒchēzhàn 火车站 train station

huódòng 活动 activity

huǒshān 火山 volcano

huòshèngzhě 获胜者 winner

huóxiàlái 活下来 to survive

huózhe 活着 to live (be alive), alive

huòzhě 或者 or

hūshì 忽视 to ignore

hùshi 护士 nurse

hútu 糊涂 confused (mentally)

húxū 胡须 beard

hùzhào 护照 passport

J

jī 鸡 chicken

jǐ 几 several

jì 系 to tie

jì 寄 to post, to mail

jì bù ... yòu bù 既不 ... 又不 neither ... nor

Jǐ ge? 几个? how many?

jǐ shí 几十 tens of, multiples of ten

jiā 加 to add

jiā 家 home, family

jiā xiāngliào de 加香料的 spicy

jiǎde 假的 false (not true)

jiǎdìng 假定 to suppose

jiàgé 价格 cost (price), tariff

jiāgōng chǔlǐ 加工处理 cured, preserved

jiājù 家具 furniture

jiǎmàode 假冒的 false (imitation)

jiān 煎 to fry

jiǎn 减 minus

jiàn 件 piece, item

jiàn 建 to build

jiàn 键 key (computer)

jiānbǎng 肩膀 shoulder

jiǎnchá 检查 to inspect, to examine

jiānchí 坚持 to stick to

jiǎndān 简单 simple (uncomplicated, modest)

jiǎndāo 剪刀 scissors

jiāndìng 坚定 firm (definite)

jiānduān 尖端 end (tip), point

jiǎnduǎn 简短 brief

jiǎnféi 减肥 to lose weight

jiāng 姜 ginger

jiǎng 讲 to speak, to tell (a story)

jiǎnghuà 讲话 speech

jiàngjià 降价 to reduce

jiǎngjià 讲价 to bargain

jiānglái 将来 in future

jiǎngshī 讲师 lecturer (at university)

jiāngyào 将要 shall, will

jiàngyóu 酱油 soy sauce

jiǎngzuò 讲座 lecture

jiānjué 坚决 determined, stubborn

jiànkāng 健康 healthy

jiànlì 建立 to establish, to set up

jiànmiàn 见面 to meet

jiànpán 键盘 keyboard (of computer)

Jiǎnpǔzhài 柬埔寨 Cambodia

Jiǎnpǔzhàide 柬埔寨的 Cambodian (in general)

Jiǎnpǔzhàirén 柬埔寨人 Cambodian (people)

Jiǎnpǔzhàiyǔ 柬埔寨语 Cambodian (language)

jiǎnqǐ 检起 to pick up, to lift (something)

jiǎnqù 减去 less, minus

jiānruì 尖锐 sharp

jiǎnruò 减弱 decline (get less)

jiǎnshǎo 减少 to decrease

jiànshēn duànliàn 健身锻炼 fitness training

jiànyì 建议 to suggest, suggestion

jiǎnzhí bù 简直不 hardly

jiànzhù 建筑 architecture

jiāo 交 to hand in

jiāo 教 to teach

jiǎo 脚 foot

jiào 叫 called, named

jiāo'ào 骄傲 proud

jiāodàizhǐ 胶带纸 tape (adhesive)

jiàohǎn 叫喊 to yell

jiāojuǎn 胶卷 film (camera)

jiāoliú 交流 to exchange (opinions)

jiǎoluò 角落 corner

jiàoshī 教师 teacher

jiàoshì 教士 priest

jiàotáng 教堂 church

jiāotōng 交通 traffic

jiàoxǐng 叫醒 awaken, wake someone up

jiāoyì 交易 to trade

jiàoyù 教育 to educate, education

jiǎozhèng 矫正 to correct

jiǎozhǐ 脚趾 toe

jiǎozi 饺子 dumpling

jiàqī 假期 vacation

jiàqián 价钱 price

jiāqín 家禽 poultry

jiārè 加热 heat, to

jiàrì 假日 holiday (vacation)

jiāshàng 加上 in addition

J

jiàshǐ 驾驶 to steer

jiàshǐ zhízhào 驾驶执照 license (for driving)

jiāyóuzhàn 加油站 petrol station

jiàzhí 价值 value (cost)

jiǎzhuāng 假装 to pretend

jīběn 基本 basic

jíbìng 疾病 disease

jìchéng 继承 to succeed

jìchéngqì 计程器 meter (in taxi)

jīchǔ 基础 base, foundation

jīdàn 鸡蛋 egg

jìde 记得 to remember

jìdu 忌妒 jealous

jídùde 极度地 extremely

Jīdùjiào 基督教 Christianity

Jīdùjiàode 基督教的 Christian (in general)

Jīdùtú 基督徒 Christian (people)

jiē 接 to pick up (someone)

jiē 街 street

jiè 借 to borrow, to lend

jiě dàbiàn 解大便 to defecate

jiē diànhuà 接电话 to answer the phone

jiě xiǎobiàn 解小便 to urinate

jiébīng 结冰 freeze

jiěchú 解除 rid: get rid of

jiěfu 姐夫 brother-in-law (wife's older sister's husband)

jiěgù 解雇 to fire someone

jièguāng 借光 excuse me! (getting past)

jiéguǒ 结果 resulting from, as a result, result

jiēhūn 结婚 marry, get married

jiějie 姐姐 sister (older)

jiējìn 接近 to approach (in space)

jiějué 解决 to resolve (a problem)

jiémù 节目 program, schedule

jiérì 节日 holiday (festival)

jièshào 介绍 to introduce someone, to present

jiēshì 揭示 to reveal

jiěshì 解释 to explain

jiēshòu 接受 to accept

jiéshù 结束 to complete, to end

jièxiàn 界线 line (mark)

jièyì 介意 mind, to be displeased

jièzhǐ 戒指 ring (jewelry)

jígé 及格 to pass (exam)

jǐge 几个 several, some

jíhé 集合 assemble, gather

jīhū 几乎 nearly, almost

jìhuà 计划 plan

jīhuāng 饥荒 famine

jīhuì 机会 chance, opportunity

jìjié 季节 season

jíliánggǔ 脊梁骨 spine

jìmò 寂寞 lonely

jīn 金 gold

jīn 筋 tendon

jǐn 紧 tight

jìn 近 close to, nearby

jìn 浸 to soak

jìn suǒ néng 尽所能 do one's best

jìnǚ 妓女 prostitute

jìnbùle hěnduō 进步了很多 get better, improve

jǐng 井 well (for water)

jǐngchá 警察 police officer

jǐngchájú 警察局 police station

jīngcháng 经常 frequent, often

jīngfèi 经费 funds, funding

jǐnggào 警告 to warn, warning

jīngguò 经过 to undergo, to go past

jīngjì 经济 economy

jīnglǐ 经理 manager

jīnglì 经历 to experience

jīnglì 精力 energy

jīngqí 惊奇 surprised

jīngquède 精确的 exact, exactly

jīngyà 惊讶 astonished

jīngyàn 经验 experience

jīngyóu 经由 via

jìngzhēng 竞争 to compete

jìngzi 镜子 mirror

jìniànbēi 纪念碑 monument

jìniànpǐn 纪念品 souvenir

jǐnjí 紧急 urgent

jǐnjǐn 仅仅 barely, merely

jìnkǒu 进口 import, to import

jìnlái 进来 come in

jìnlù 进路 way in

jìnpào 浸泡 to soak, to immerse

jìnrù 进入 to enter

jǐnshēn duǎnchènkù 紧身短衬裤 panties

jīnshǔ 金属 metal

jīnshǔxiàn 金属线 wire

jīntiān 今天 today

jīnwǎn 今晚 tonight

jìnyībùde 进一步的 further, additional

jǐnzhāngde 紧张的 tense

jìnzhǐ 禁止 prohibit

jìpǐn 祭品 sacrifice

jīròu 肌肉 muscle

jíshǎo 极少 few

jǐshí 几时 when

jìsuàn 计算 calculate

jìsuànqì 计算器 calculator

jiǔ 九 nine

jiǔ 久 long (time)

jiǔ 酒 liquor, alcohol

jiù 旧 old (of things)

jiù lái 就来 on the way

jiǔbā 酒吧 bar (serving drinks)

jiūfēn 纠纷 dispute

jiùfù 舅父 uncle (mother's brother)

jiùhùchē 救护车 ambulance

jiùjiu 舅舅 uncle (mother's brother)

Jiùmìng a! 救命啊 Help!

jiùmǔ 舅母 aunt (wife of mother's older/younger brother)

jiùsǎo 舅嫂 sister-in-law (wife of one's older/younger brother)

jiǔshí 九十 ninety

Jiǔyuè 九月 September

jiùzhěn 就诊 consultation (by doctor)

jìxiàlái 记下来 to note down

jíxiǎode 极小的 tiny

jīxiè 机械 machine, machinery

jìxù 继续 to continue

jìzhě 记者 reporter, journalist

jízhěn 急诊 emergency

jízhōng 集中 to concentrate

juǎnrù jiūfēn 卷入纠纷 involved

juǎnxīncài 卷心菜 cabbage

jùdàde 巨大的 huge

jué 嚼 to chew

juésè 角色 role

juéde 觉得 to feel

juédìng 决定 to decide, decision

jùhào 句号 period (end of a sentence)

jùhuì 聚会 party (event)

jǔjué 咀嚼 to chew

jùjué 拒绝 to refuse, refusal

jùlí 距离 distance

jūmín 居民 resident, inhabitant

jūnduì 军队 army

jùyuàn 剧院 theater (drama)

júzi 桔子 orange (citrus)

jùzi 句子 sentence

júzizhī 桔子汁 orange juice

K

kǎchē 卡车 truck

kāfēi 咖啡 coffee

kāi 开 to turn on, to switch on, to open

kāi wánxiào 开玩笑 to joke

kāichē 开车 to drive (a car), leave (train/bus)

kāichuán 开船 to sail

kāiduān 开端 beginning

kāigān 揩干 to wipe

kāiguān 开关 switch

kāile 开了 on (turned on)

kāiqiāng 开枪 to shoot

K

kāishǐ 开始 to begin, to start, beginning

kāishuǐ 开水 boiled water

kāitóu 开头 beginning

kāixīn 开心 happy

kāizhǎn 开展 to develop

kāizuì 开罪 to offend

kàn 看 to look, to see, to watch (movie)

kànbìng 看病 consultation (by doctor)

kànbudǒng 看不懂 not able to understand (by reading)

kànbujiàn 看不见 can't see

kànbuqīngchu 看不清楚 can't see clearly

kàndedǒng 看得懂 able to understand (by reading)

kàndeqīngchu 看得清楚 can see clearly

kàndǒngle 看懂了 understood (by reading)

kāngfù 康复 recover from an injury or illness

kāngkǎide 慷慨的 generous

kàngshēngsù 抗生素 antibiotics

kānguǎn 看管 look after, watch over, guard

kàngyì 抗议 to protest

kànjiàn 看见 to see

kànshàngqù 看上去 to look, to seem, to appear

kànshū 看书 to read

kǎo 烤 to bake, to roast, to grill

kàojìn 靠近 close to, nearby

kǎolǜ 考虑 to consider, to think over

kǎolú 烤炉 oven

kǎoshì 考试 exam, test

kǎoyā 烤鸭 roast duck

kě 渴 thirsty

kè 课 lesson

kě huòdé de 可获得的 available

kě'ài 可爱 cute, appealing, lovely

kèbóde 刻薄的 mean (cruel)

kèfú 克服 to overcome

kělián 可怜 pity

kěndìng 肯定 sure

kěnéng 可能 perhaps, probably, possible

kěnéngde 可能地 possibly

kěnqiú 恳求 to plead

kěpà 可怕 terrible

kèren 客人 guest

kèshàng 刻上 to engrave

késou 咳嗽 to cough

késou yàoshuǐ 咳嗽药水 cough syrup

késoushēng 咳嗽声 cough

kěxī 可惜 what a pity!

kēxué 科学 science

kěyǐ 可以 can, be able to

kěyòngde 可用的 to make available

kèzhàn 客栈 lodge, small hotel

kōngde 空的 empty

kōngdì 空地 field, empty space

kònggào 控告 to accuse

kǒnghè 恐吓 to threaten

kōngjiān 空间 space

kǒngjù 恐惧 fear

kōngqì 空气 air

kōngqì wūrǎn 空气污染 air pollution

kōngtiáo 空调 air conditioning

kòngzhì 控制 hold back

kǒudài 口袋 pocket

kǒuyìyuán 口译员 interpreter

kū 哭 to cry

kuài 快 fast, rapid, quick

kuài! 快！come on, let's go

kuài dào le 快到了 on the way

kuài diǎnr 快点儿 hurry up!

kuàizi 筷子 chopsticks

kuān 宽 wide

kuānchang 宽敞 spacious

kuāndù 宽度 width

kuàngquánshuǐ 矿泉水 mineral water

L

kuángrè àihàozhě 狂热爱好者 fan (admirer)

kuānshù 宽恕 forgiveness, mercy

kǔde 苦的 bitter

kùn 困 tired (sleepy)

kùnnan 困难 difficult

kuòdà 扩大 to enlarge

kūqì 哭泣 to weep

kùzi 裤子 trousers, pant

L

lā 拉 to pull

là 蜡 wax

là 辣 hot (spicy)

lǔchéng 旅程 trip, journey

lǚguǎn 旅馆 hotel

lái 来 to come

lái yuèjīng 来月经 to menstruate

láihuípiào 来回票 return ticket

láilín 来临 to approach (in time)

láiyuán (yú) 来源 (于) to originate, to come from

lājī 垃圾 garbage

làjiāo 辣椒 pepper (chilli)

làjiāojiàng 辣椒酱 chilli sauce

lǎnduò 懒惰 lazy

lánqiú 篮球 basketball

lánsè 蓝色 blue

lánzi 篮子 basket

lǎo 老 old (of persons)

lǎobǎn 老板 boss

lǎohǔ 老虎 tiger

láojià 劳驾 excuse me! (attracting attention)

lǎolao 姥姥 grandmother (maternal)

lǎoshī 老师 teacher

lǎoshǔ 老鼠 rat

Lǎowō 老挝 Laos

Lǎowōde 老挝的 Laotian (in general)

Lǎowōrén 老挝人 Laotian (people)

Lǎowōyǔ 老挝语 Laotian (language)

lǎoye 老爷 grandfather (maternal)

lāxià 拉下 leave behind by accident

làzhú 蜡烛 candle

lèi 累 **tired** (worn out)

lèihuàile 累坏了 exhausted

lěng 冷 cold

lěngquè 冷却 to cool

lèshì 乐事 treat (something special)

lí 梨 pear

lián 连 even (also)

liǎn 脸 face

liáng 量 to measure

liǎng 两 two (measure)

liàng 亮 light (bright)

liǎng cì 两次 twice

liǎng ge 两个 both

liànggān 晾干 dry out (in the sun)

liánghǎo zhùyuàn 良好祝愿 best wishes

liángkuài 凉快 cool

liángxié 凉鞋 sandals

liǎngzhě dōu bù 两者都不 neither

liánhuānhuì 联欢会 party (event)

liánjiē 连接 to connect together

liánjiēdiǎn 连接点 connection (transport)

liánjiēqǐlái 连接起来 to join together

liànrǔ 炼乳 condensed milk

liánxì 联系 contact, connection

liànxí 练习 to practise, practice

liányīqún 连衣裙 dress, frock

Liáoguó 寮国 Laos

Liáoguóde 寮国的 Laotian (in general)

Liáoguórén 寮国人 Laotian (people)

L

Liáoguóyǔ 寮国语 Laotian (language)

liǎojiě 了解 to realize, be aware of

liáotiānr 聊天儿 chat

líbā 篱笆 fence

lǐbài 礼拜 week

Lǐbài'èr 礼拜二 Tuesday

Lǐbàiliù 礼拜六 Saturday

Lǐbàisān 礼拜三 Wednesday

Lǐbàisì 礼拜四 Thursday

Lǐbàitiān 礼拜天 Sunday

Lǐbàiwǔ 礼拜五 Friday

Lǐbàiyī 礼拜一 Monday

lièjiǔ 烈酒 spirits, hard liquor

lièkāile 裂开了 cracked

lǐfàdiàn 理发店 barber

líhūn 离婚 to divorce

líkāi 离开 to depart

lìkè 立刻 immediately

lílehūn 离了婚 divorced

lìliang 力量 force, power, strength

lǐmiàn 里面 inside

límíng 黎明 dawn

líng 零 zero

lìng rén wéinán de 令人为难的 embarrassing

lìng rén xīngfèn de 令人兴奋的 exciting

lìng rén yúkuàide 令人愉快的 pleasant

lǐngdài 领带 tie, necktie

lǐngdǎo 领导 lead (to be a leader)

lǐngdǎorén 领导人 leader

língjiàn 零件 part (of machine)

língqián 零钱 change, small

lǐngshìguǎn 领事馆 consulate

lìngwài 另外 other (alternative)

línjū 邻居 neighbor

línyùjiān 淋浴间 shower (for washing)

lìrú 例如 such as, for example

lìrùn 利润 profit

lìshǐ 历史 history

lǐtáng 礼堂 hall

liú 留 to keep

liù 六 six

liúcún 留存 leave behind for safekeeping

liúlì 流利 fluent

liùshí 六十 sixty

liúsù 留宿 to stay overnight

liúxià 留下 to stay, to leave behind on purpose

liúxíng 流行 popular

liúxuè 流血 bleed

liúyán 留言 message

liúyánjī 留言机 answering machine

liúyì 留意 pay attention

Liùyuè 六月 June

lǐwù 礼物 present (gift)

lìxī 利息 interest (bank)

lìzhī 荔枝 lychee

lǐzi 李子 plum

lìzi 例子 example

lóngde 聋的 deaf

lóu 楼 story (of a building)

lóushàng 楼上 upstairs

lòushuǐ 漏水 to leak

lóutī 楼梯 stairs

lóutīng 楼厅 circle (theater seats)

lóuxià 楼下 downstairs

lù 路 road

luàn-qī bā-zāo 乱七八糟 in a mess

lùbiāo 路标 road sign

lùjūn 陆军 army

lǚkè 旅客 traveler

lúnzi 轮子 wheel

luòhòu 落后 backward

luósīdāo 螺丝刀 screwdriver

luǒtǐde 裸体的 naked, nude

luòxià 落下 to fall

luòxiàlái 落下来 to fall

luóxuánxíngde 螺旋形的 spiral

lǜsè 绿色 green

lǜshī 律师 lawyer

lùtú 路途 journey

lùxiàn 路线 lane (of a highway)
lùxiàngdài 录象带 video cassette
lùxiàngjī 录象机 VCR, video recorder
lǚxíng 旅行 to travel, trip, journey
lǚxíng 履行 fulfill
lùyīn 录音 tape recording
lǚyóu zhǐnán 旅游指南 guidebook
lǚyóuzhě 旅游者 tourist, traveler
lúzi 炉子 cooker, stove

M

(yī) mǐ （一）米 meter
mǎ 马 horse
mǎchē 马车 cart (horsecart)
máfan 麻烦 trouble
máfande 麻烦的 troublesome
mǎi 买 to buy
mài 卖 to sell
mǎi dōngxi 买东西 to shop, to go shopping
màidiào 卖掉 sold
màiwán 卖完 sold out
májiàng 麻将 mahjong
Mǎláixīyà 马来西亚 Malaysia
Mǎláixīyàde 马来西亚的 Malaysian (in general)
Mǎláixīyàrén 马来西亚人 Malaysian (people)
māma 妈妈 mother
mámùde 麻木的 numb
mǎn 满 full
màn 慢 slow
máng 忙 busy (doing something)
mángguǒ 芒果 mango
mànmānde 慢慢地 slowly
mǎnyì 满意 to satisfy
mǎnyìde 满意的 satisfied
mǎnzú 满足 to satisfy
māo 猫 cat
máojīn 毛巾 towel

màopáihuò 冒牌货 false (imitation)
máoxiàn 毛线 wool
máoyī 毛衣 jumper, sweater
màoyì 贸易 trade
màozi 帽子 hat
mǎshàng 马上 at once
máyóu 麻油 sesame oil
měi 每 each, every
měi 美 beautiful
měi cì 每次 every time
méi gǎnshàng 没赶上 to miss (bus, flight)
měi ge dìfang 每个地方 everywhere
měi ge rén 每个人 everybody, everyone
měi jiàn shì 每件事 everything
měi nián de 每年的 annual
měi yè de 每夜的 nightly
méi yìsi 没意思 boring
měi zhōu 每周 weekly
mèifu 妹夫 brother-in-law (wife's younger sister's husband)
méiguānxi 没关系 never mind!
Měiguó 美国 United States
Měiguóde 美国的 American (in general)
Měiguórén 美国人 American (people)
měihǎo 美好 pretty (of places, things)
měilì 美丽 pretty (of places, things)
mèimei 妹妹 sister (younger)
méiyǒu 没有 no, not, without
méiyǒu shénme 没有什么 nothing
mén 门 door
mèn 闷 dull (boring)
mèng 梦 dream
mí 迷 fan (admirer)
miànbāo 面包 bread
miánbù 棉布 cotton
Miǎndiàn 缅甸 Burma
Miǎndiànde 缅甸的 Burmese (in general)

M

Miǎndiànrén 缅甸人 Burmese (people)

Miǎndiànyǔ 缅甸语 Burmese (language)

miànduì 面对 to face, to stand up to

miǎnfèi 免费 free of charge

miànfěn 面粉 flour

miánhuā 棉花 cotton wool

miànjiá 面颊 cheek

miànjù 面具 mask

miàntiáo 面条 noodles

miǎo 秒 second (instant)

miáoshù 描述 to describe

miáotiáode 苗条的 slender

mǐfàn 米饭 rice (cooked)

míhóutáo 猕猴桃 kiwi fruit

míhuò 迷惑 puzzled

mílù 迷路 lost (can't find way)

mìmì 秘密 secret

míng jiào 名叫 called, named

míngbai 明白 understand

míngdān 名单 list

míngliàng 明亮 bright

mìnglìng 命令 to order, to command, command

míngnián 明年 next year

míngpái 名牌 brand name

míngquède 明确的 definite

míngshèng 名胜 place of interest

míngtiān 明天 tomorrow

míngxiǎnde 明显地 apparently

míngxìnpiàn 明信片 postcard

míngzhì 明智 sensible

míngzi 名字 name, given name

mínzú fúzhuāng 民族服装 costume

mínzúde 民族的 national

mìshū 秘书 secretary

mō 摸 to touch

mófǎng 模仿 to copy someone or something

mógu 蘑菇 mushrooms

mòshēngrén 陌生人 stranger

mòshuǐ 墨水 ink

mótuōchē 摩托车 motorcycle

mǒu ge dìfang 某个地方 somewhere

mǒuchù 某处 somewhere

mùdì 目的 goal, purpose

mùdìdì 目的地 destination

mùlù 目录 list

mùqiánde 目前的 at the present moment

mǔqin 母亲 mother

mùshī 牧师 priest

Mùsīlín 穆斯林 Muslim

mùtou 木头 wood

mùzhìde 木制的 wooden

N

ná 拿 to bring

nǎ (ge) 哪（个）which?

nà 那 that

nǎ yī zhǒng? 哪一种？ what kind of?

nǚ'ér 女儿 daughter

nàbiān 那边 over there, there

nǎilào 奶酪 cheese

nǎinai 奶奶 grandmother (paternal)

nàixīn 耐心 patient (calm)

nálái 拿来 to bring

nǎli 哪里 where

nàli 那里 there

nánbiān 南边 south

nándé 难得 rarely, seldom

nánguò 难过 sad

nánháir 男孩儿 boy

nánkàn 难看 ugly

nánpéngyou 男朋友 boyfriend

nánrén 男人 man

nánwéiqíng 难为情 embarrassing

nánxìng 男性 male

nǎo 脑 brain

nǎozi 脑子 mind, brain

nǎr 哪儿 where

nàr 那儿 there

nǎr dōu bú zài 哪儿都不在 nowhere

nàxiē 那些 those
názǒu 拿走 to take, to remove
nèicún 内存 RAM (computer)
nèidì 内弟 brother-in-law
  (wife's younger brother)
nèijiù 内疚 to feel guilty
nèikù 内裤 underpants
nèixiōng 内兄 brother-in-law
  (wife's older brother)
nèiyī 内衣 underwear,
  undershirt
néng 能 can, may
nénglì 能力 ability
ní 泥 mud
nǐ 你 you
Nǐ hǎo 你好 hello, hi
nǐ hǎo ma 你好吗 how are
  you?
nǐ kàn 你看 look!
nián 年 year
niánlíng 年龄 age
niánqīng 年轻 young
niánqīngrén 年轻人 youth
niǎo 鸟 bird
niǎocháo 鸟巢 nest
nílóng 尼龙 nylon
nǐmen 你们 you (plural)
nín 您 you (polite)
níngkě 宁可 rather than
níngméng 柠檬 lemon,
  citrus
nítǔ 泥土 earth, soil
niú 牛 cow
niúnǎi 牛奶 milk
niúròu 牛肉 beef
nóng 浓 thick (of liquids)
nòng gānjìng 弄干净 to clean
nòng hútu 弄糊涂 confused
  (mentally)
nòngcuò 弄错 mistaken
nònggān 弄干 to dry
nònghuài 弄坏 break, shatter
nǚ chènshān 女衬衫 blouse
nǚde 女的 female
nǚfú 女服 dress, frock
nǚhái 女孩 girl
nǚlì 努力 effort
nuòmǐ 糯米 glutinous rice

nǚpéngyou 女朋友 girlfriend
nǚrén 女人 woman
nǚshén 女神 goddess
nǚshì 女士 lady
nǚwáng 女王 queen
nǚxu 女婿 son-in-law

O

ǒu'ěr 偶尔 rarely, seldom
ǒurán 偶然 by chance
ǒuránde 偶然的 accidentally,
  by chance
ǒutù 呕吐 to be sick (vomit)
Ōuzhōu 欧洲 Europe

P

pá 扒 to pickpocket
pà 怕 afraid
páichéng yīxiàn 排成一线
  to line up
páichì 排斥 bar (blocking way)
páiduì 排队 to queue, to line up
pāimài 拍卖 to auction
pāimàidiào 拍卖掉 auctioned
  off
páizhào 牌照 license, permit
pāndēng 攀登 to climb up
  (hills, mountains)
pàng 胖 fat, plump
pángbiān 旁边 next to, side
pángxiè 螃蟹 crab
pánzi 盘子 dish, plate
pǎo 跑 to run
pāoqì 抛弃 to desert, to
  abandon
páshàng 爬上 climb onto
páshǒu 扒手 pickpocket
péi 陪 to accompany
pèi'ǒu 配偶 spouse
péngliáo 棚寮 shack
pēngtiáo 烹调 cooking,
  cuisine
péngwū 棚屋 hut, shack
péngyou 朋友 friend

P

péngzhàng 膨胀 expand, grow larger
pēntì 喷嚏 sneeze
pēnwùqì 喷雾器 spray
piàn 骗 to cheat
piànkè 片刻 moment (instant)
piányi 便宜 inexpensive, cheap
piànzi 骗子 someone who cheats
piào 票 ticket
piàojià 票价 fare
piàoliang 漂亮 pretty (of women)
pífū 皮肤 skin
pígé 皮革 leather
pìgu 屁股 buttocks
píjuànde 疲倦的 weary
píng 平 level (even, flat)
píngděng 平等 equality
píngděngde 平等的 equal
píngguǒ 苹果 apple
pínghuá 平滑 even (smooth)
pínghuáde 平滑的 smooth (of surfaces)
píngjī 评击 attack (with words)
píngjìng 平静 calm, still, quiet
píngjūn 平均 average (numbers)
píngmù 屏幕 screen (of computer)
píngtǎnde 平坦的 flat, smooth
píngyuán 平原 plain (level ground)
píngzi 瓶子 bottle
pínjíde 贫瘠的 barren
pīnxiě 拼写 to spell
pīnyīn 拼音 combine sounds into syllables
píyǐngxì 皮影戏 shadow play
pòhuài 破坏 to damage
pǔbiànde 普遍地 generally
pùbù 瀑布 waterfall
pùkèpái 扑克牌 cards, game
pǔshíde 朴实的 modest, simple
pǔsù 朴素 plain (not fancy)
pútao 葡萄 grapes
pútaojiǔ 葡萄酒 wine
pǔtōngde 普通的 common, frequent
Pǔtōnghuà 普通话 Mandarin (language)

Q

qī 七 seven
qí 旗 flag
qǐ fǎnyìng 起反应 to react
qí zìxíngchē 骑自行车 ride, to (bicycle)
qǐ zuòyòng 起作用 to function, to work
qiān 千 thousand
qián 钱 money
qiǎn 浅 shallow
qiàn 欠 to owe
qiánbāo 钱包 wallet, purse
qiānbǐ 铅笔 pencil
qiánbì 钱币 currency
qiáng 墙 wall
qiángdàde 强大的 powerful
qiǎngjiù 抢救 to rescue
qiángpò 强迫 force, compel
qiángzhìxìngde 强制性的 compulsory
qiángzhuàng 强壮 strong
qiánjìn 前进 advance, go forward
qiánmiàn 前面 front
qiānmíng 签名 to sign, signature
qiántiān 前天 day before yesterday
qiānwàn 千万 ten million
qiānxū 谦虚 modest, simple
qiānzhèng 签证 visa
qiáo 桥 bridge
qiào 俏 pretty (of women)
qiāodǎ 敲打 to beat, to strike
qiǎokèlì 巧克力 chocolate
qiāomén 敲门 to knock
qìchē 汽车 car, automobile
qìchēzhàn 汽车站 bus station

qǐchuáng 起床 get up (from bed)

qídǎo 祈祷 to pray, prayer

qǐdòng 起动 to start (machines)

qiézi 茄子 eggplant

qìfēn 气氛 atmosphere, ambience

qǐgài 乞丐 beggar

qíguài 奇怪 strange

qìhòu 气候 climate

qímǎ 骑马 ride, to (horse)

qǐmǎ 起码 at least

qíncài 芹菜 celery

qínfèn 勤奋 hardworking, industrious

qīng 轻 light (not heavy)

qǐng 请 please

qīngchu 清楚 clear

qīngjié 清洁 cleanliness

qíngkuàng 情况 situation, how things are

qínglǎng 晴朗 sunny

qínglǐ 情理 reason

qīngnián 青年 youth (young person)

qǐngqiú 请求 to request

qīngshàonián 青少年 teenager

qīngtāng 清汤 soup (clear)

qīngtóng 青铜 bronze

qǐngwèn 请问 excuse me! (attracting attention)

qíngxù 情绪 emotion

qīngzǎo 清早 early in the morning

Qīngzhēn 清真 Muslim

Qīngzhēnjiào 清真教 Islam

Qīngzhēnjiàode 清真教的 Islamic

Qīngzhēnjiàotú 清真教徒 Muslim (people)

Qīngzhēnsì 清真寺 mosque

qīngzhǒng 青肿 bruise

qìngzhù 庆祝 to celebrate

qīnpèi 钦佩 to admire

qīnqi 亲戚 relatives, family

qīnyǎn mùdǔ 亲眼目睹 to witness

qīnzuǐ 亲嘴 kiss

qióng 穷 poor (not rich)

qīpiàn 欺骗 to deceive

qīshí 七十 seventy

qíshí 其实 actually

qìshuǐ 汽水 soft drink

qítā 其他 other

qítède 奇特的 fancy

qǐtú 企图 attempt

qiū 丘 hill

qiú 球 ball

qiūtiān 秋天 autumn

qīwàng 期望 to expect

qìyóu 汽油 petrol, gasoline

qìyóuzhàn 汽油站 petrol station

qǐyuán 起源 origin

qìyuē 契约 contract

Qīyuè 七月 July

qīzi 妻子 wife

qǐzi 起子 screwdriver

qǔ 取 to fetch

qù 去 to go

qù nǎli 去哪里 where to?

quàn'gào 劝告 advice

quánbù 全部 complete (whole)

quánbùde 全部的 entirety, whole

quánbùde 全部地 completely

quánjǐng 全景 panorama

quánlì 权力 authority (power)

quánlì 权利 rights

quánmiànde 全面的 general, all-purpose

quánwēi 权威 authority (person in charge)

qùdiào 去掉 to get rid of

quēdiǎn 缺点 defect

quēdiàode 缺掉的 missing (absent)

quèdìng 确定 sure

quēfáde 缺乏的 scarce

quèqiè 确切 exact, exactly

quèrèn 确认 to confirm

quēshǎo 缺少 lacking

quēxí 缺席 absent

qùgòujì 去垢剂 detergent

Q

qùguo 去过 to have been somewhere
qùnián 去年 last year
qúnzi 裙子 skirt
qǔxiāo 取消 to cancel
qǔxiào 取笑 to laugh at

R

rán'ér 然而 nevertheless
ràng 让 let, allow
ràng mǒurén dāchē 让某人搭车 lift (ride in car)
ránhòu 然后 then
rè 热 hot (temperature)
rén 人 people, person
réncí 仁慈 forgiveness, mercy, kind
rènde 认得 to recognize
rēng 扔 to throw
rēngdiào 扔掉 to throw away, to throw out
réngōngde 人工的 artificial
réngrán 仍然 still, even now
rènhé dìfang 任何地方 anywhere
rènhé rén 任何人 anybody, anyone
rènhé shì 任何事 anything
rènhé yī ge 任何一个 either
rénkǒu 人口 population
rénqíng 人情 human feelings
rénqíngwèi 人情味 human touch
rènshi 认识 to know, to be acquainted with
rènwéi 认为 to reckon, to have an opinion
Rìběn 日本 Japan
Rìběnde 日本的 Japanese (in general)
Rìběnrén 日本人 Japanese (people)
rìchángde 日常的 daily
rìchéngbiǎo 日程表 itinerary
rìchū 日出 sunrise
rìjì 日记 diary

rìluò 日落 sunset
rìqī 日期 date (of the month)
Rìyǔ 日语 Japanese (language)
róngqià 融洽 harmonious
róngxǔ 容许 allowed to
róngyì 容易 simple (easy)
ròu 肉 meat
ròutāng 肉汤 broth, soup
ròuwán 肉丸 meatball
ruǎn 软 soft
ruǎnjiàn 软件 software (computer)
rúcǐ 如此 such
rǔfáng 乳房 breasts
rúguǒ 如果 if
Rújiào 儒教 Confucianism
Rújiāsīxiǎng 儒家思想 Confucianism
rùkǒu 入口 entrance, way in
rǔlào 乳酪 cheese
rùnhóutáng 润喉糖 cough lolly
ruò 弱 weak
rǔzhào 乳罩 bra

S

(shǔyú) ... de (属于) ... 的 of, from
sāhuǎng 撒谎 lie, tell a falsehood
sāizi 塞子 plug (bath)
sān 三 three
sǎn 伞 umbrella
sānfēnzhīyī 三分之一 third (1/3)
sàngfū 丧夫 widowed
sàngqī 丧妻 widower
sānjiǎokù 三角裤 briefs
sānjiǎoxíng 三角形 triangle
sānshí 三十 thirty
Sānyuè 三月 March
sànzhuāngde 散装的 loose (not in packet)
sǎo 扫 sweep, to
sāoluàn 骚乱 disturbance
sàozhou 扫帚 broom

săozi 嫂子 sister-in-law
(wife of husband's older brother)

sēnlín 森林 forest

shā 杀 to kill

shāfā 沙发 couch, sofa

shāmò 沙漠 desert (arid land)

shān 山 mountain

shăndiàn 闪电 lightning

shāndǐng 山顶 peak, summit

shàng xīngqī 上星期 last week

shàngchē 上车 to board
(bus, train)

Shàngdì 上帝 God

shāngdiàn 商店 shop, store

shānghài 伤害 to hurt, injury

Shànghǎi 上海 Shanghai

shāngháng 商行 firm, company

shāngkǒu 伤口 cut (injury),
wound

shāngliang 商量 discuss

shàngmiàn 上面 above

shàngqù 上去 to go up, to
climb

shāngrén 商人 businessperson

shàngshēng 上升 to rise, to
ascend

shāngǔ 山谷 valley

shǎnguāngdēng 闪光灯 flash
(camera)

shàngwǎng kāfēiguǎn
上网咖啡馆 Internet café

shàngwǎng qù chōnglàng
上网去冲浪 surfing on the
Internet

shàngwèi 尚未 not yet

shāngyè 商业 business

shānhú 珊瑚 coral

shānlán 栅栏 fence

shānpō 山坡 slope

shānyáng 山羊 goat

shànzi 扇子 fan (for cooling)

shāo 烧 to burn

shǎo 少 few

shāohuǐ 烧毁 burned down

shāokǎo 烧烤 to grill

shǎoliàngde 少量的 small
amount

shāoshāng 烧伤 burn (injury)

shāotā 烧塌 burned down,
out

shāowēi 稍微 slightly

sháozi 勺子 spoon

shāyú 鲨鱼 shark

shāzhù 刹住 brake, to brake

shāzi 沙子 sand

shé 蛇 snake

shéi/shuí 谁 who?

shèjí 涉及 to involve

shèjídào 涉及到 involved

shèlùjī 摄录机 video recorder

shēn 深 deep

shén 神 god

shèn 肾 kidney

shēn'gāo 身高 height
(body)

Shéndào 神道 Shinto

shénfù 神父 priest

shēng 生 to give birth

shēngchǎn 生产 to produce

shèngdàde 盛大的 great,
impressive

shēngde 生的 raw, uncooked,
rare

shēnghuó 生活 life, live
(be alive)

shēngmìng 生命 life

shēngqì 生气 cross, angry,
annoyed

shēngrì 生日 birthday

shēngrì kuàilè 生日快乐
happy birthday!

shèngxiàde 剩下的 remainder,
leftover

shēngyīn 声音 sound,
noise, voice

shèngyúde 剩余的 rest,
remainder

shéngzi 绳子 string, rope

shénhuà 神话 myth

shénjīngbìng 神经病 crazy

shénme 什么 what? pardon
me? what did you say?

shénme dìfang 什么地方
somewhere

shénme shíhou 什么时候
when

27

S

shénmǔ 婶母 aunt (wife of father's younger brother)
shēnqǐng 申请 to apply
shénshèng 神圣 holy
shénshèngde 神圣的 sacred
shēntǐ 身体 body
shēnyè 深夜 late at night
shèshì 摄氏 centigrade
shétou 舌头 tongue
shèxiàng 摄像 to videotape
shèxiàngdài 摄像带 video cassette
shí 十 ten
shǐ 屎 shit
shì 是 be, exist
shì 试 to try
shǐ rén nánkān 使人难堪 embarrassing
shǐ téngtòng 使疼痛 to ache
shǐ xiànrù 使陷入 to involve
shí yì 十亿 billion
shí'èr 十二 twelve
Shí'èryuè 十二月 December
shībài 失败 failure
shìbīng 士兵 soldier
shìchǎng 市场 market
shìchuān 试穿 try on (clothes)
shìdàngde 适当的 appropriate
shīde 湿的 wet
shìde 是的 yes, indeed!
shìfàng 释放 to release
shìgù 事故 accident
shìhéde 适合的 fitting, suitable
shíhuì 实惠 economical
shíjì 实际 really (in fact)
shìjì 世纪 century
shíjiān 时间 time
shìjiàn 事件 happening, incident, event
shìjiè 世界 world
shíkè 时刻 point (in time)
shíkèbiǎo 时刻表 timetable, schedule
shìmín 市民 citizen
shípǔ 食谱 recipe
shíqī 时期 period (of time)
shìqíng 事情 matter, issue

shìqū 市区 downtown
shísān 十三 thirteen
shìshí 事实 fact
shísì 十四 fourteen
shítou 石头 rock, stone
shíwàn 十万 hundred thousand
shīwàng 失望 disappointed
shíwǔ 十五 fifteen
shíwù 食物 food
shìwù 事物 thing
shīwù zhāolǐngchù 失物招领处 lost property
shìxiān 事先 earlier, beforehand
shìxiàng 事项 item, individual thing
shìyàn 试验 test
shìyàng 式样 pattern, design
shīyè 失业 unemployed
shíyī 十一 eleven
shìyìng 适应 to adapt to an new environment
shìyīshì 试衣室 fitting room
Shíyīyuè 十一月 November
Shíyuè 十月 October
shìzhèn 市镇 town
shízhōng 时钟 clock
shìzhōngxīn 市中心 center of city
shízhuāng biǎoyǎn 时装表演 fashion show
shízìlùkǒu 十字路口 crossroads, intersection
shīzōngle 失踪了 missing (lost person)
shǒu 手 hand
shòu 瘦 thin (of persons)
shòu huānyíng 受欢迎 popular
shòu míhuò 受迷惑 puzzled
shòu tòngkǔ 受痛苦 to suffer
shōudào 收到 to receive
shóude 熟的 ripe, cooked
shǒudiàntǒng 手电筒 flashlight, torch
shōufèi 收费 fee
shǒugōngyìpǐn 手工艺品 handicraft

shòuhuòyuán 售货员 sales assistant

shōují 收集 to gather

shōujù 收据 receipt

shōukuǎn 收款 to collect payment

shòushāng 受伤 hurt (injured)

shōushí 收拾 tidy up

shǒushì 首饰 jewelry

shǒutíbāo 手提包 briefcase

shǒutuīchē 手推车 cart (pushcart)

shǒuwàn 手腕 wrist

shóuxī 熟悉 familiar with

shòuxiǎode 瘦小的 slight

shōuyīnjī 收音机 radio

shǒuyìrén 手艺人 craftsperson

shǒuzhāi 守斋 to fast

shǒuzhǐ 手指 finger

shǒuzhuó 手镯 bracelet

shū 书 book

shū 输 to lose, to be defeated

shǔ 数 count

shù 树 tree

shuā 刷 to brush

shuāidǎo 摔倒 fall over

shuāngbèi 双倍 double

shuǎngkǒu 爽口 delicious

shuāzi 刷子 brush

shǔbiāo 鼠标 mouse (computer)

shūcài 蔬菜 vegetable

shúde 熟的 ripe

shūfǎ 书法 calligraphy

shūfu 舒服 comfortable

shūfù 叔父 uncle (father's younger brother)

shuǐ 水 water

shuǐguǒ 水果 fruit

shuìjiào 睡觉 to sleep

shuǐniú 水牛 buffalo (water buffalo)

shuǐtǒng 水桶 bucket

shuìyī 睡衣 nightclothes, pyjamas

shuìzhe 睡着 asleep

shùjǐn 束紧 to tie

shùjù lùxiàngjī 数据录象机 DVD

shúliànde 熟练的 skillful

shùliàng 数量 amount

shūmǔ 叔母 aunt (wife of father's younger brother)

shùnbiàn wèn yīxià 顺便问一下 by the way

shùnlì 顺利 to go smoothly

shùnlù bàifǎng 顺路拜访 to stop by, to pay a visit

shuō 说 to speak, to say

shuōhuǎng 说谎 to lie, to tell a falsehood

shūqián 输钱 to lose money

shúrén 熟人 acquaintance

shūshu 叔叔 uncle (father's younger brother)

shǔyú 属于 belong to

shūzhuō 书桌 desk

shūzi 梳子 comb

shùzi 数字 figure, number

sǐ 死 to die

sì 四 four

sīchóu 丝绸 silk

sīdài 丝带 ribbon

sìfēnzhīyī 四分之一 quarter

sìhū 似乎 to seem

sījī 司机 driver

sǐjī 死机 crashed (computer)

sīkāi 撕开 to rip open

sǐle 死了 dead

sīrénde 私人的 private

sìshí 四十 forty

sǐwáng 死亡 death

sīxiǎng 思想 thoughts

sìyuàn 寺院 temple (Chinese)

Sìyuè 四月 April

sòng 送 to send

sōngdòngde 松动的 loose (wobbly)

suān 酸 sour

suàn 算 count

suānjú 酸桔 lime, citrus

suànpán 算盘 abacus

suāntián 酸甜 sweet and sour

suāntòng 酸痛 sore, painful

S

sùdù 速度 speed
Sūgélán 苏格兰 Scotland
Sūgélánde 苏格兰的 Scottish (in general)
Sūgélánrén 苏格兰人 Scots
suì 岁 years old
suìpiàn 碎片 piece, portion, section
suīrán 虽然 although, though
sùliào 塑料 plastic
sùliàodài 塑料袋 plastic bag
sǔnhuài 损坏 to damage
sūnnǚ 孙女 granddaughter (son's daughter)
sūnzi 孙子 grandson (son's son)
suǒ 锁 lock
suǒshàng 锁上 to lock
suǒyǐ 所以 so, therefore
suǒyǒu 所有 possessions
suǒyǒuwù 所有物 belongings
suǒzhù 锁住 locked

T

tā 他 he, him
tā 她 she, her
tǎ 塔 tower
tāde 他的 his
tāde 她的 her, hers
tài 太 too (excessive)
tài duō 太多 too much
tàidu 态度 attitude
táifēng 台风 typhoon
Tàiguó 泰国 Thailand
Tàiguóde 泰国的 Thai (in general)
táijiē 台阶 steps, stairs
tàitai 太太 madam (term of address), Mrs
tàiyáng 太阳 sun
Tàiyǔ 泰语 Thai (language)
tāmen 他们 they, them
tāmende 他们的 their, theirs
tāng 汤 soup (spicy stew)
táng 糖 sugar
tàng 烫 to iron (clothing)

tángcù 糖醋 sweet and sour
tángguǒ 糖果 sweets, candy
tǎngxià 躺下 to lie down
tánhuà 谈话 to talk
tánhuáng 弹簧 spring (metal part)
tánlùn 谈论 talk about
tānzi 摊子 stall (of vendor)
tǎnzi 毯子 blanket
tào 套 set
tǎolùn 讨论 to discuss, discussion
táopǎo 逃跑 run away
táozi 桃子 peach
tèbié 特别 special
tèbiéde 特别地 especially
tèdiǎn 特点 characteristic
tí 提 to carry
tiān 天 day
tián 甜 sweet
tiǎn 舔 to lick
tián jiàngyóu 甜酱油 soy sauce (sweet)
tiánbiǎo 填表 to fill out (form)
tiānhuābǎn 天花板 ceiling
tiānkōng 天空 sky
tiānpíng 天平 scales
tiānqì 天气 weather
tiānqì yùbào 天气预报 weather forecast
tiánshí 甜食 sweet, dessert
Tiānzhǔjiào 天主教 Catholic
Tiānzhǔjiàode 天主教的 Catholic (in general)
Tiānzhǔjiàotú 天主教徒 Catholic (people)
tiào 跳 to jump
tiáojiàn 条件 condition (subjective/objective)
tiáokuǎn 条款 item, individual thing
tiáowèizhī 调味汁 sauce
tiàowǔ 跳舞 to dance
tiāoxuǎn 挑选 to select, to pick, to choose
tiǎozhàn 挑战 challenge
tídào 提到 to mention
tiě 铁 iron (metal)

tiědào 铁道 railroad, railway
tiělù 铁路 railroad, railway
tígāo 提高 raise, lift
tígōng 提供 offering
tímù 题目 topic
tīng 听 to listen
tíng 停 to stop, to cease
tīngbudǒng 听不懂 not able to understand (by hearing)
tīngbujiàn 听不见 didn't hear
tīngbuqīngchu 听不清楚 heard unclearly
tíngchē 停车 to park (car)
tīngdedǒng 听得懂 able to understand (by hearing)
tīngdǒngle 听懂了 understood (by hearing)
tīnghuà 听话 obedient
tīngjiàn 听见 to hear
tíngzhǐ 停止 to stop, to halt
tíqǐ 提起 to lift, to raise
tǐwēn 体温 temperature (body)
tíxǐng 提醒 to remind
tǐyàn 体验 to experience
tǐzhòng 体重 body weight
tīzi 梯子 ladder
tóng 铜 bronze, copper
tòng 痛 sore, painful
tōngcháng 通常 normal, normally
tóngchuáng 童床 cot
tōngguò 通过 through, past
tòngkǔ 痛苦 suffering
tóngshí 同时 meanwhile
tóngshì 同事 co-worker, colleague
tōngxìn 通信 to correspond (write letters)
tóngyàng 同样 identical
tóngyàngde 同样地 likewise
tóngyì 同意 to agree
tóngyīde 同一的 identical
tōngzhī 通知 to inform, notice
tóngzhì 同志 comrade
tōu 偷 to steal

tóu 头 head
tōu qiánbāo 偷钱包 to pickpocket
tóufa 头发 hair
tóujīn 头巾 headdress
tóupiào 投票 to vote
tóusù 投诉 to complain, complaint
tóuténg 头疼 have a headache
tóutòng 头痛 have a headache
tóuxián 头衔 title (of person)
tóuyūn 头晕 dizzy
tú 图 drawing
tuántǐ 团体 group
tūchū 突出 to stick out
tuī 推 to push
tuǐ 腿 leg
tuīchí 推迟 to postpone, to delay
tuījiàn 推荐 to recommend
tuìxiū 退休 retired
tūn 吞 to swallow
tuō 脱 to take off (clothes)
tuōpán 托盘 tray
tuōxié 拖鞋 slippers
tuǒyuánxíngde 椭圆形的 oval (shape)
tūrán 突然 suddenly
túshūguǎn 图书馆 library
tūtóude 秃头的 bald
tǔzhùde 土著的 indigenous (in general)
tǔzhùrén 土著人 indigenous

W

wàiguóde 外国的 foreign
wàiguórén 外国人 foreigner
wàimào 外貌 appearance, looks
wàimiàn 外面 outside
wàishēng 外甥 nephew (maternal)
wàishēngnǚ 外甥女 niece (maternal)
wàisūnnǚ 外孙女 granddaughter (maternal)

wàisūnzi 外孙子 grandson (maternal)

wàitào 外套 jacket

wàiyī 外衣 coat, jacket

wàizǔfù 外祖父 grandfather (maternal)

wàizǔfùmǔ 外祖父母 grandparents (maternal)

wàizǔmǔ 外祖母 grandmother (maternal)

wǎn 晚 late at night

wǎn 碗 bowl

wàn 万 ten thousand

wánchéng 完成 to complete (finish)

wǎndiǎn 晚点 delayed (train, bus etc)

wāndòu 豌豆 peas

wǎnfàn 晚饭 dinner, evening meal

wǎng 网 net

wǎng 往 to, toward (a place)

wǎngcháng 往常 usual

wàngjì 忘记 to forget

wàngle 忘了 forgotten

wǎngqiú 网球 tennis

wángùde 顽固的 stubborn, determined

wǎngluò 网络 network

wǎngzhàn 网站 website

wánjiéle 完结了 finished (complete)

wánjù 玩具 toy

wánle 完了 over, finished

wánpíde 顽皮的 naughty

wánquán 完全 completely

wánr 玩儿 to play, to have fun

wǎnshang 晚上 evening

wànwàn 万万 hundred million

wàzi 袜子 socks

wéi/wèi 喂 hello! (on phone)

wèi 为 for

wèi 喂 to feed

wèi ... fúwù 为 ... 服务 to serve

wèi ... nǐdìng de 为 ... 拟定的 intended for ...

Wēi'ěrsī 威尔斯 Wales

Wēi'ěrsīde 威尔斯的 Welsh (in general)

Wēi'ěrsīrén 威尔斯人 Welsh (people)

Wēi'ěrsīyǔ 威尔斯语 Welsh (language)

wěiba 尾巴 tail

wèichéngshúde 未成熟的 unripe

wěidà 伟大 great, impressive

wèidànde 味淡的 mild (not spicy)

wèidào 味道 taste, flavor

wèihūnfū 未婚夫 fiancé

wèihūnqī 未婚妻 fiancée

wèijīng 味精 MSG

wèishénme 为什么 why? what for?

wēixiǎn 危险 danger

wēixiǎn de 危险的 dangerous

wēixíngde 微型的 mini

wéiyī 唯一 sole, only

wèiyú 位于 to be situated, to be located

wén 闻 to smell

wěn 吻 kiss

wèn 问 to enquire, to ask about

wēndù 温度 temperature (heat)

wènhòu 问候 greetings

wénhuà 文化 culture

wénjiàn 文件 document, letter

wénjù 文具 stationery

wēnnuǎn 温暖 warmth

wēnnuǎnde 温暖的 mild (not cold)

wēnquán 温泉 hot spring

wēnróude 温柔的 mild (not severe)

wèntí 问题 question, problem

wénxué 文学 literature

wényǎde 文雅的 gentle

wénzhāng 文章 article (in newspaper)

wénzi 蚊子 mosquito

wǒ 我 I, me

wǒde tiān 我的天 goodness!

wǒde 我的 my, mine

wǒmen 我们 we, us

wǒmende 我们的 our, ours

wòshì 卧室 bedroom

wū 屋 room (in house)

wǔ 五 five

wù 雾 fog

wūdiǎn 污点 stain

wūdǐng 屋顶 roof

wǔfàn 午饭 lunch, midday meal

wūgòu 污垢 dirt, filth

wūguī 乌龟 turtle (land)

wǔhuì 舞会 dance

wùhuì 误会 misunderstanding

wùjiě 误解 mistaken

wúlǐ 无礼 impolite

wúliáo 无聊 bored

wúlùn héshí 无论何时 whenever

wùpǐn 物品 item, individual thing

wǔqì 武器 weapon

wūrǎn 污染 pollution

wūrǔ 侮辱 to insult

wǔshí 五十 fifty

wúxiànzhì 无限制 free of restraints

wǔyè 午夜 midnight

wúyòngde 无用的 useless

Wǔyuè 五月 May

wúzhī 无知 ignorant

X

xī 吸 to suck

xī 稀 thin (of liquids)

xǐ 洗 to wash

xǐ ge línyù 洗个淋浴 to take a shower

xǐ'ài 喜爱 to prefer

xī'nán 西南 south-west

xiā 虾 prawn

xià 下 down, downward

xià dìngdān 下订单 to order something

xià yī ge 下一个 next (in line, sequence)

xià'è 下颚 lower jaw

xiàba 下巴 chin

xiàchē 下车 get off (bus/train)

xiàchuán 下船 get off (boat)

xià fēijī 下飞机 get off (plane)

xiàhu 吓唬 frightened

xiàjiàng 下降 to decline (get less)

xiálù 狭路 lane (alley)

xiān 先 first, earlier, beforehand

xián 咸 salty

xiàn 线 thread

xián bǐnggān 咸饼干 cracker, salty biscuit

xián jiàngyóu 咸酱油 soy sauce (salty)

xiàndàide 现代的 modern

xiāng 香 incense, fragrant

xiāng 箱 box

xiǎng 想 to think, to ponder

xiàng 向 toward

xiàng 巷 alley, lane

xiàng 象 to look like

xiàng ... tí yìjiàn 向 ... 提意见 to advise

xiàng qián 向前 forward

xiàng zhè zhǒng de 象这种的 such as, for example

xiāngbīnjiǔ 香槟酒 champagne

xiāngdāng 相当 quite (fairly)

xiǎngfa 想法 thoughts

xiāngfǎn 相反 opposite (contrary)

Xiānggǎng 香港 Hong Kong

xiānggé 相隔 apart

xiāngjiāo 香蕉 banana

xiàngjiāo 橡胶 rubber (material)

xiàngliàn 项链 necklace

xiāngliào 香料 spices

xiāngmáo 香茅 lemon grass

xiǎngniàn 想念 to miss (loved one)

X

xiàngpícā 橡皮擦 rubber (eraser)

xiàngqí 象棋 Chinese chess

xiàngshàng 向上 up, upward

xiāngshí de rén 相识的人 acquaintance

xiǎngshòu 享受 to enjoy

xiāngshuǐ 香水 perfume

xiāngsìde 相似的 similar

xiāngtóng 相同 alike

xiāngxià 乡下 country (rural area)

xiàngxià 向下 down, downward

xiǎngxiàng 想象 to imagine, to fancy

xiāngxiàng 相象 to resemble

xiāngxìn 相信 to believe

xiàngyá 象牙 ivory

xiāngyān 香烟 cigarette

xiāngzhuàng 相撞 to collide

xiāngzi 箱子 suitcase, chest (box)

xiānjué tiáojiàn 先决条件 condition (pre-condition)

xiànkuǎn 现款 cash, money

xiànmù 羡慕 envy

xiānsheng 先生 Mr (term of address)

xiǎnshìqì 显示器 monitor (of computer)

xiànzài 现在 now, nowadays, presently

xiànzhù 陷住 stuck, won't move

xiǎo 小 little (small)

xiào 笑 to smile, to laugh

xiǎobiàn 小便 to urinate

xiǎodiànzi 小垫子 mat

xiǎofèi 小费 tip (gratuity)

xiàoguǒ 效果 effect, result

xiǎohái 小孩 child (young person)

xiàohuà 笑话 joke

xiǎohúzi 小胡子 moustache

xiǎojie 小姐 Miss (term of address)

xiǎokāng 小康 well off, wealthy

xiǎolǚguǎn 小旅馆 lodge, small hotel

xiǎolǎoshǔ 小老鼠 mouse (animal)

xiǎoqì 小气 mean (stingy)

xiāoqiǎn 消遣 pastime

xiǎorénwù 小人物 nobody

xiǎoshān 小山 hill

xiǎoshí 小时 hour

xiǎoshū 小叔 brother-in-law (husband's younger brother)

xiǎoshuō 小说 novel

xiǎotiánbǐng 小甜饼 cookie, sweet biscuit

xiǎotōu 小偷 pickpocket

xiǎoxiā 小虾 shrimp, prawn

xiǎoxīn 小心 careful!

xiǎoxīnde 小心的 cautious

xiàtiān 夏天 summer

xiàwǔ 下午 afternoon (3 pm to dusk)

xiàxīngqī 下星期 next week

xiàxuě 下雪 to snow

xiàyǔ 下雨 to rain

xiázhǎi 狭窄 narrow

xīběi 西北 north-west

xībiān 西边 west

xìchángde 细长的 slim

xié 鞋 shoes

xiě 写 to write

xié'ède 邪恶的 wicked

xiédìng 协定 agreement

xiēwēi 些微 slight

xièxie 谢谢 thank you

xiézhù 协助 assistance, to assist

xiězuò 写作 composition, writings

xǐfàjì 洗发剂 shampoo

Xīfāngde 西方的 Western

Xīfāngrén 西方人 Westerner

xífù 媳妇 daughter-in-law

xīgài 膝盖 knee

xīguā 西瓜 watermelon

xíguàn 习惯 used to

xīhóngshì 西红柿 tomato

xǐhuan 喜欢 to be fond of

xīhuǒ 熄火 to stall (car)

xīlánhuācài 西兰花菜 broccoli

xīmiè 熄灭 go out (fire, candle)

xīn 新 new

xìn 信 to mail, to post, letter

xìnfēng 信封 envelope

xíng 行 okay

xǐng 醒 awake

xìng 姓 surname

xìngbié 性别 sex, gender

xíngchéng 形成 to form shape

xíngdòng 行动 action

xīngfèn 兴奋 excited

xìnggé 性格 character (personality)

xìng xíngwéi 性行为 sex, sexual activity

xǐnglái 醒来 awake, wake up

xíngli 行李 baggage, luggage

xìngmíng 姓名 name

xīngqī 星期 week

Xīngqī'èr 星期二 Tuesday

Xīngqīliù 星期六 Saturday

Xīngqīrì 星期日 Sunday

Xīngqīsān 星期三 Wednesday

Xīngqīsì 星期四 Thursday

Xīngqītiān 星期天 Sunday

Xīngqīwǔ 星期五 Friday

Xīngqīyī 星期一 Monday

xīngxīng 星星 star

xìngyùnde 幸运地 luckily, fortunately

xìngyùnde 幸运的 lucky

xíngzhuàng 形状 shape

Xīnjiāpō 新加坡 Singapore

Xīnjiāpōde 新加坡的 Singaporean (in general)

Xīnjiāpōrén 新加坡人 Singaporean (people)

xīnláng 新郎 bridegroom

xīnnián hǎo 新年好 happy new year!

xīnniáng 新娘 bride

xìnrèn 信任 to trust

xīnwén 新闻 news

xīnwénjiè 新闻界 press, journalism

xìnxī 信息 information

xīnxiān 新鲜 fresh

Xīnxīlán 新西兰 New Zealand

Xīnxīlánde 新西兰的 things pertaining to New Zealand

Xīnxīlánrén 新西兰人 New Zealander

xìnxīn 信心 confidence

xìnyǎng 信仰 belief, faith

xìnyòngkǎ 信用卡 credit card

xīnzàng 心脏 heart

xiōngdìjiěmèi 兄弟姐妹 siblings

xiōngměngde 凶猛的 fierce

xiōngqiāng 胸腔 chest (breast)

xīshēng 牺牲 to sacrifice

xǐshǒujiān 洗手间 restroom, bathroom

xísú 习俗 custom, tradition

xiūbǔ 修补 to mend

xiūchēháng 修车行 garage (for repairs)

xiūchǐ 羞耻 shame, disgrace

xiùhuāde 绣花的 embroidered

xiūjiàtiān 休假天 day off

xiūlǐ 修理 to repair

xiūxi 休息 rest, to relax

xǐwǎn 洗碗 to wash the dishes

xīwàng 希望 to wish, to hope

xīyǐn 吸引 to attract

xīyǒude 稀有的 rare (scarce)

xǐzǎo 洗澡 to bathe, to take a bath

xìzhuāng 戏装 costume

xuǎnjǔ 选举 election

xuǎnzé 选择 to choose, choice

xǔduō 许多 lots of

xué 学 to learn, to study

xuě 雪 snow

xuè 血 blood

xuéfèi 学费 fee

xuèguǎn 血管 blood vessel

xuějiā(yān) 雪茄(烟) cigar

xuésheng 学生 student, pupil

xuéxí 学习 to learn

xuéxiào 学校 school

xuèyā 血压 blood pressure

xūgòu 虚构 to make up, to invent

X

xŭkězhèng 许可证 permit
xúnfúde 驯服的 tame
xùnliàn 训练 training
xúnwènchù 询问处 information
　desk
xúnzhǎo 寻找 to search for
xūyào 需要 to need, need

Y

(yī chē) huòwù （一车）货物
　load
... yàng de rén? ... 样的人?
　one who, the one which
yā 压 press, to
yá 牙 tooth, teeth
yágāo 牙膏 toothpaste
yājīn 押金 advance money,
　deposit
yālì 压力 pressure
yān 烟 smoke
yán 盐 salt
yán'gé 严格 strict, severe
yǎnchū 演出 performance
yándòng 岩洞 cave
yáng 羊 sheep
yàngběn 样本 sample
yángcōng 洋葱 onion
yángguāng 阳光 sunlight
yángròu 羊肉 lamb, mutton
yángmáo 羊毛 wool
yǎngyù 养育 bring up (children)
yàngzi 样子 appearance
yānhuā 烟花 fireworks
yànhuì 宴会 banquet
yǎnjiǎng 演讲 speech, to
　make a
yǎnjing 眼睛 eye
yǎnjìng 眼镜 glasses,
　spectacles
yánjiū 研究 research
yǎnlèi 眼泪 tears
yánlì 严厉 severe
yǎnméi 眼眉 eyebrow
yānnì 淹溺 to drown
yánqī 延期 to postpone
yánsè 颜色 color

yānshuǐ 淹水 flood
yǎnshuō 演说 speech,
　to make a
yānsǐ 淹死 to drown
yánsù 严肃 serious (not funny)
yànwù 厌恶 to dislike
yànwùde 厌恶的 disgusting
yánzhe 沿着 to follow along
yánzhòng 严重 serious (severe)
yáo 摇 to shake
yǎo 咬 to bite
yào 要 to want, to request
yào 药 drug (medicine)
yáobǎi 摇摆 to swing
yàobùrán 要不然 else, or else
yāodài 腰带 belt
yàodiàn 药店 pharmacy,
　drugstore
yàofāng 药方 prescription
yàofáng 药房 drugstore,
　pharmacy
yáohuǎng 摇晃 to shake
　something
yàopiàn 药片 pills, tablets
yāoqǐng 邀请 to invite,
　invitation
yāoqiú 要求 to demand, to
　request
yàoshi 要是 if
yàoshi 钥匙 key (to room)
yàowǎn 药丸 pills
yáshuā 牙刷 toothbrush
yǎzhìde 雅致的 elegant
Yàzhōu 亚洲 Asia
Yàzhōude 亚洲的 Asian (in
　general)
Yàzhōurén 亚洲人 Asian
　(people)
yāzi 鸭子 duck
yě 也 as well, also
yè 页 page
yè 夜 night
yě shì 也是 too (also)
yěbù 也不 nor
yěshēngde 野生的 wild
yěxǔ 也许 maybe, perhaps
yéye 爷爷 grandfather
　(paternal)

Y

yēzi 椰子 coconut
yèzi 叶子 leaf
yèzǒnghuì 夜总会 nightclub
yī 一 one
yì 亿 hundred million
yī cì 一次 once
yī dá 一打 dozen
yī fān fēng shùn 一帆风顺 bon voyage!
yī fèn 一份 portion, serve
yǐ fùkuǎn 已付款 paid
yī ge rén 一个人 alone
yī shuāng 一双 pair of, a
yī tào xīfú 一套西服 suit, business
yìbān 一般 average (so-so, just okay)
yíbàn 一半 half
yíbèizi 一辈子 lifetime
yíbùfèn 一部分 partly
Yìdàlì 意大利 Italy
Yìdàlìde 意大利的 Italian (in general)
Yìdàlìrén 意大利人 Italian (people)
Yìdàlìyǔ 意大利语 Italian (language)
yìdiǎn búcuò 一点不错 exactly! just so!
yìdiǎnr 一点儿 little (not much)
yídìng 一定 sure, certain
yídòng diànhuà 移动电话 mobile phone
yīfu 衣服 clothes, clothing
yífu 姨夫 uncle (husband of mother's sister)
yígòng 一共 altogether, in total
yíhàn 遗憾 regret
yíhànde 遗憾地 regrettably
yíhuǐr 一会儿 later
yǐhūn 已婚 married
yìjiàn yīzhì 意见一致 agreed!
yìjiàn 意见 opinion, advice
yíjiāo 移交 to hand over
yíjiě 姨姐 sister-in-law (wife's older sister)
yǐjīng 已经 already
yīkào 依靠 to depend on

yīliáo 医疗 medical
yímèi 姨妹 sister-in-law (wife's younger sister)
yīmèir dìzhǐ 依妹儿地址 email address
yīmèir 依妹儿 email (message)
yímǔ 姨母 aunt (wife's mother's older/younger sister)
yín 银 silver
yīn'àn 阴暗 dull (weather)
yǐncáng 隐藏 hidden
yīncǐ 因此 therefore
yīndào 阴道 vagina
Yìndù 印度 India
Yìndùde 印度的 Indian (in general)
Yìndùníxīyà 印度尼西亚 Indonesia
Yìndùrén 印度人 Indian (people)
Yìndùyǔ 印度语 Indian (language)
yíng 赢 to win
yīng'ér 婴儿 baby
yīng'érchuáng 婴儿床 cot
yìngbì 硬币 coin
yìngde 硬的 stiff
yīnggāi 应该 ought to
Yīngguó 英国 England, United Kingdom
Yīngguóde 英国的 British (in general)
Yīngguórén 英国人 English (people)
yíngjiù 营救 to rescue
yīngjùn 英俊 handsome
yìngpán 硬盘 hard disk/drive (computer)
Yīngtèwǎng 英特网 Internet
Yīngwén 英文 English (language)
yǐngxiǎng 影响 to affect, to influence
yǐngxiǎnglì 影响力 influence
Yīngyǔ 英语 English (language)
yìngzhǐbǎn 硬纸版 cardboard
yǐngzi 影子 shadow
yínháng 银行 bank (finance)

Y

yīnjīng 阴茎 penis
yīnliángchù 阴凉处 shade
yǐnliào 饮料 drink, refreshment
Yìnní 印尼 Indonesia
Yìnníde 印尼的 Indonesian
(in general)
Yìnnírén 印尼人 Indonesian
(people)
Yìnníyǔ 印尼语 Indonesian
(language)
yǐnqǐ xiànmù de 引起羡慕的
envious
yīntiān 阴天 overcast, cloudy
yīnwèi 因为 because
yìnxiàng 印象 impression
yǐnxíng yǎnjìng 隐型眼镜
contact lens
yīnyuè 音乐 music
yīnyuèhuì 音乐会 concert
yīnyuètīng 音乐厅 concert
hall
yīqǐ 一起 together
yǐqián 以前 ago, before
(in time)
yīqiè 一切 everything
yīshēng 医生 doctor
yìshí 意识 awareness
yìshídào 意识到 aware
yìshù 艺术 art
yìshùjiā 艺术家 artist
yìsi 意思 meaning
Yīsīlánjiào 伊斯兰教 Islam
Yīsīlánjiàode 伊斯兰教的
Islamic
yìtú 意图 intention
yǐxià 以下 following
yīxiē 一些 some, a little
yíxīn 疑心 suspicion
yīyàng 一样 same
yīyuàn 医院 hospital
Yīyuè 一月 January
yīzhí 一直 straight ahead
yǐzhì 以致 in order that, so that
yìzhì 抑制 to restrain
yǐzi 椅子 chair
yòng 用 to use, by means of
yòng zìmǔ pīnxiě 用字母拼写
to spell

yōngbào 拥抱 to embrace
yǒnggǎn 勇敢 brave, daring
yònggōng 用功 hardworking,
industrious
yòngguāngle 用光了 finished
(none left)
yōngjǐ 拥挤 busy (crowded)
yǒngjiǔde 永久的 permanent
yòngrén 佣人 servant
yòngyì 用意 to mean (intend)
yōngyǒu 拥有 to own
yǒngyuǎn 永远 for ever
yóu 油 oil
yǒu 有 there is, there are
yòu ... yòu 又 ... 又
both ... and
yǒu bāndiǎn de 有斑点的
spotted (pattern)
yǒu lǐmào de 有礼貌的 well-
mannered
yǒu nénglì 有能力 to be
capable of
yǒu rénqíngwèi de 有人情味
的 human
yǒu xìnxīn 有信心 to have
confidence
yǒu xīwàng de 有希望地
hopefully
yǒu xīyǐnlì de 有吸引力的
attractive
yǒu yìsi 有意思 interesting
yǒu zhìxù de 有秩序地
orderly, organized
yòubiān 右边 right-hand side
yǒubìngde 有病的 ill, sick
yǒudúde 有毒的 poisonous
yǒuguān 有关 about
(regarding), concerning
yǒuhǎo 友好 friendly
yōuhuì 优惠 discount
yóujú 邮局 post office
yóukè 游客 tourist
yōuměi 优美 beautiful
(of places)
yǒumíng 有名 famous
yōumòde 幽默的 humorous
yóunì 油腻 fat, grease
yóupiào 邮票 stamp (postage)

yóuqī 油漆 to paint (house, furniture), paint

yǒuqián 有钱 well off, wealthy

yóuqíshì 尤其是 particularly, especially

yǒuqù 有趣 interesting

yǒurén 有人 somebody, someone

yòurén 诱人 attractive

yǒushí 有时 sometimes

yǒutiáowénde 有条纹的 striped

yóuxì 游戏 game

yǒuxiào 有效 valid

yōuxiùde 优秀的 excellent

yóuyǒng 游泳 to swim

yǒuyòng 有用 useful

yóuyǒngchí 游泳池 swimming pool

yóuyǒngyī 游泳衣 swimming costume

yóuyú 鱿鱼 squid

yóuzhá 油炸 fried

yǒuzīyǒuwèide 有滋有味的 tasty

yǒuzuì 有罪 guilty (of a crime)

yú 于 on (of dates)

yú 鱼 fish

yǔ 雨 rain

yǔ ... xiāngbǐ 与 ... 相比 compared with

yuǎn 远 far

yuánliàng 原谅 to forgive

yuánquān 圆圈 circle

yuánrén 猿人 ape

yuànwàng 愿望 desire

yuánxíngde 圆形的 round (shape)

yuányīn 原因 reason, cause

yuánzhūbǐ 圆珠笔 ballpoint pen

yuànzi 院子 courtyard

yùdìng 预定 to reserve (ask for in advance)

yuè 月 month

yuēdìng 约定 to fix (a time, appointment)

yuèfù 岳父 father-in-law (wife's father)

yuèguò 越过 to go past

yuēhǎo 约好 to fix (a time, appointment)

yuèjīngqī 月经期 period (menstrual)

yuèliang 月亮 moon

yuèmǔ 岳母 mother-in-law (wife's mother)

Yuènán 越南 Vietnam

Yuènánde 越南的 Vietnamese (in general)

Yuènánrén 越南人 Vietnamese (people)

Yuènányǔ 越南语 Vietnamese (language)

yuèqì 乐器 musical instrument

yùfùkuǎn 预付款 advance money, deposit

yùgāng 浴缸 bathtub

yúkuàide 愉快的 enjoyable

yúlù 鱼露 fish sauce

yùmǐ 玉米 corn, grain

yùn yīfu 熨衣服 to iron (clothing)

yùndòng 运动 sports

yùndǒu 熨斗 iron (for clothing)

yùnqì 运气 luck

yùnsòng 运送 to deliver

yǔnxǔ 允许 to allow, to permit

yùpén 浴盆 bathtub

yúshì 于是 thus, so

yùshì 浴室 bathroom

yǔyán 语言 language

yùyī 浴衣 bathrobe

yùyuē 预约 appointment

Z

zài 在 at

zài 再 again

zài 载 to carry

zài ... de qiánmiàn 在 ... 的前面 in front of ...

zài ... dǐxià 在 ... 底下 under

Z

zài ... duìmiàn 在 ... 对面
across from ...
zài ... hòumiàn 在 ... 后面
behind ...
zài ... lǐ 在 ... 里 inside of
zài ... pángbiān 在 ... 旁边
beside ...
zài ... qījiān 在 ... 期间 during
zài ... shàng 在 ... 上 on ...,
at ...
zài ... wài 在 ... 外 outside
zài ... wàimiàn 在 ... 外面
outside of ...
zài ... yǐhòu 在 ... 以后 after ...
zài ... zhè yīdài. 在 ... 这一带
around ... (nearby)
zài ... zhīzhōng 在 ... 之中
among ...
zài ... zhījiān 在 ... 之间
between ...
zài ... zhōuwéi 在 ... 周围
around ... (surrounding)
zài jiā 在家 at home
zài nǎli/nǎr 在哪里／哪儿
where
zài qínglǐ zhī nèi 在情理之内
within reason
zài yī (ge) 再一（个）another
one (same again)
zàijiàn 再见 goodbye
zāinàn 灾难 disaster
zànchéng 赞成 agreed!
zāng 脏 dirty
zànglǐ 葬礼 funeral
zánmen 咱们 we, us
(includes the one addressed)
zánmende 咱们的 our
(includes the one addressed)
zànshí 暂时 temporary
zànyáng 赞扬 praise
zāo 糟 bad
zǎo 早 early
zǎofàn 早饭 breakfast,
morning meal
zǎorì kāngfù 早日康复 get
well soon!
zǎoshang 早上 morning
zàoyīn 噪音 noise

zázhì 杂志 magazine
zéguài 责怪 to blame
zéi 贼 thief
zēngjiā 增加 to rise, to increase
zēngjiā tǐzhòng 增加体重
to gain weight
zēngzhǎng 增长 grow larger, to
zěnme 怎么 how?
zérèn 责任 duty (responsibility)
zhài 债 debt
zhāijiè 斋戒 to fast
zhàn 站 to stand, stop
(bus, train)
zhàndòu 战斗 battle
zhǎng 长 grow, be growing
(plant)
zhàng'ài 障碍 hindrance
zhǎngbèi 长辈 elder
zhǎngdà 长大 grow up (child)
zhàngdān 帐单 bill
zhàngfu 丈夫 husband
zhǎnlǎn 展览 display
zhǎnxiàn 展现 to reveal
(make visible)
zhànxiàn 占线 engaged
(telephone)
zhànxìngde 粘性的 sticky
zhànyǒu 占有 to possess
zhànzhēng 战争 war
zhǎo 找 to look for, to seek
zhàogu 照顾 to take care of
zhàoguǎn 照管 to take care of
zháohuǒ 着火 on fire
zhàojiàn 召见 to call, to
summon
zhāopái 招牌 signboard
zhàopiàn 照片 photograph
zhāoshǒu 招手 to wave
zhàoxiàng 照相 to photograph
zhàoxiàngjī 照相机 camera
zhè 这 this
zhédié 折叠 to fold
zhéduàn 折断 to break apart
zhéduànle 折断了 broken,
snapped (of bones, etc.)
zhèlǐ 这里 here
zhème, nàme 这么，那么 so
(degree)

zhēn 针 needle
zhēn diūliǎn! 真丢脸 shame: what a shame!
zhēnchéngde 真诚的 truly
zhēnde 真的 really (in fact), true
zhēnde ma? 真的吗 ? really?
zhēng 争 fight over, to
zhèng 挣 to earn
zhěng ge 整个 whole, to be complete
zhèngcháng 正常 normal
zhèngchángde 正常地 normal, normally
zhēngchǎo 争吵 to argue
zhèngdǎng 政党 party (political)
zhēngde 蒸的 steamed
zhèngfāngxíng 正方形 square (shape)
zhèngfǔ 政府 government
zhěngjié 整洁 tidy
zhèngjù 证据 proof
zhēngliúshuǐ 蒸馏水 distilled water
zhēnglùn 争论 argument
zhèngmíng 证明 to prove
zhēngqì 蒸汽 steam
zhěngqí 整齐 tidy
zhèngquè 正确 right, correct
zhèngrén 证人 witness
zhèngshìde 正式的 official, formal
zhèngshū 证书 certificate
zhěngtǐ lái kàn 整体来看 on the whole
zhèngzhì 政治 politics
zhēnjūn 真菌 fungus
zhěntou 枕头 pillow
zhènyǔ 阵雨 shower (of rain)
zhēnzhū 珍珠 pearl
zhèr 这儿 here
zhètáng 蔗糖 sugarcane
zhèxiē 这些 these
zhèyàng 这样 thus, so
zhèyàngde 这样的 such
zhǐ 只 just, only
zhǐ 纸 paper
zhì 炙 grill, to

zhí'ér 侄儿 nephew (paternal)
zhīchí 支持 to back up
zhǐchū 指出 point out
zhīdao 知道 to know (be aware of)
zhídào 直到 until
zhíde 直的 straight (not crooked)
zhíde 值得 to be worth, value, good
zhīfù 支付 payment
zhǐhuī 指挥 to command
zhǐjiǎ 指甲 nail (finger, toe)
zhìliáo 治疗 to treat (medically)
zhīmá 芝麻 sesame seeds
zhínǚ 侄女 niece (paternal)
zhīqián 之前 beforehand, earlier
zhìshǎo 至少 at least
zhīshi 知识 knowledge
zhǐshì 只是 sole, only
zhǐshì 指示 instruct, tell to do something
zhǐtòngyào 止痛药 painkiller
zhíwù 植物 plant
zhíwùyuán 植物园 botanic gardens
zhìxù 秩序 order
zhíyè 职业 occupation, profession
zhǐyǒu 只有 only
zhìzào 制造 to manufacture
zhǐzé 指责 accuse, to
zhǐzhāng 纸张 sheet (of paper)
zhízhào 执照 license, permit
zhízi 侄子 nephew (paternal)
zhōng 钟 clock
zhòng 种 to plant
zhòng 重 heavy
zhōng/xiǎoxuéshēng 中／小学生 schoolchild
Zhōngguó 中国 China

Zhōngguóde 中国的 Chinese (in general)

Zhōngguórén 中国人 Chinese (people)

zhōngjiān 中间 center, middle

zhǒnglèi 种类 sort, type

zhòngliàng 重量 weight

zhòngshì 重视 to value

zhōngtóu 钟头 hour

Zhōngwén 中文 Chinese (language)

zhōngwǔ 中午 midday, afternoon

zhōngyāng 中央 central

zhòngyào 重要 important, importance

zhòngyàode 重要的 major (important)

zhōngyú 忠于 to stick to

zhōngyú 终于 finally

zhòngzhí 种植 to grow, to cultivate

zhōngzhǐ 终止 to end (finish)

zhōngzhuǎnzhàn 中转站 connection (transport)

zhǒngzi 种子 seed

zhōu 洲 continent

zhǒu 肘 elbow

zhòuméi 皱眉 frown

zhōumò 周末 weekend

zhōuqīxìng piāntóutòng 周期性偏头痛 migraine

zhōuwéi de shìwù 周围的事物 surroundings

zhū 猪 pig

zhǔ 煮 to boil

zhù 住 to stay, to live

zhù 柱 post, column

zhù hǎo 祝好 best wishes

zhù nǐ hǎoyùn 祝你好运 good luck!

zhuǎn 转 to turn around

zhuǎnchē 转车 to change bus/train

zhuàngchē 撞车 crashed (car)

zhuānghuò 装货 to load up

zhuāngmǎn 装满 to fill

zhuāngpèi 装配 to assemble, to put together

zhuāngshì 装饰 to decorate

zhuàngshí 壮实 stout

zhuāngshìpǐn 装饰品 ornament

zhuàngtài 状态 condition (status)

zhuānjiā 专家 expert

zhuànqián 赚钱 to make money (in business)

zhuāzhe 抓着 to hold, to grasp

zhuāzhù 抓住 to catch

zhūbǎo 珠宝 jewelry

zhǔdetòude 煮得透的 well-cooked, well-done

zhùdiàn 住店 check in

zhùdiàn shǒuxù 住店手续 check in formalities

zhǔfèile 煮沸了 boiled

zhùhè nǐ 祝贺你 congratulations!

zhuī 追 to chase

zhuīqiú 追求 to seek, to pursue

zhuīqiú xiǎngshòu 追求享受 play around

zhǔjī 主机 computer (main)

zhújiànde 逐渐地 gradually

zhǔnbèi 准备 to prepare, to get ready

zhǔnbèihǎole 准备好了 prepared, ready

zhǔnshí 准时 on time

zhǔnxǔ 准许 to permit, to allow

zhuōbù 桌布 tablecloth

zhuólù 着陆 to land (plane)

zhuōzi 桌子 table

zhǔrén 主人 host

zhūròu 猪肉 pork

zhùrù 注入 to inject

zhǔshóule 煮熟了 cooked

zhùsù 住宿 accommodations

zhǔyào 主要 main, most important

zhǔyàode 主要的 mainly

Z

zhŭyi 主意 idea
zhùyì 注意 to notice, look out!
zìcóng 自从 since
zìdiǎn 字典 dictionary
zīgé 资格 qualification
zǐgōng 子宫 uterus
zìháo 自豪 pride
zìjǐ 自己 self
zìjǐ 自给 self-sufficient
zìjǐde 自己的 own, personal
zìmǔ 字母 alphabet
zìrán fēngjǐng 自然风景 scenery
zìránde 自然的 natural
zìránjiè 自然界 nature
zǐsè 紫色 purple
zīshì 姿势 gesture
zǐtóng 紫铜 copper
zìwǒ jièshào 自我介绍 to introduce oneself
zìxíngchē 自行车 bicycle
zìyóu 自由 freedom
zìyóude 自由的 free, independent
zìzūn 自尊 self-respect, self-esteem
zìzūnxīn 自尊心 pride
zōngjiào 宗教 religion
zǒnglǐ 总理 prime minister
zōngsè 棕色 brown
zǒngshì 总是 always
zǒngtǒng 总统 president
zǒu 走 leave, depart
zǒudédào de jùlí 走得到的距离 walking distance
zǒuláng 走廊 corridor
zǒulù 走路 on foot
zǒuzī 走私 to smuggle (illegal goods)
zū 租 to hire, to rent
zǔ'ài 阻碍 to hinder
zuànshí 钻石 diamond
zǔfù 祖父 grandfather (paternal)
zǔfùmǔ 祖父母 grandparents (paternal)
zúgòu 足够 enough

zuǐ 嘴 mouth
zuì 最 most (superlative)
zuì hǎo 最好 best
zuìchūde 最初的 original
zuǐchún 嘴唇 lips
zuìduō 最多 most (the most of)
zuìfàn 罪犯 criminal
zuìhòu 最后 last (final)
zuìhòude 最后的 finally
zuìhuàide 最坏的 worst
zuìshǎo 最少 least (smallest amount)
zǔmǔ 祖母 grandmother (paternal)
zūnjìng 尊敬 to respect
zūnyán 尊严 respect
zūnzhòng 尊重 respect
zuò 坐 to sit
zuò 做 to act, to make
zuò báirìmèng 做白日梦 to daydream
zuò huǒchē 坐火车 by rail
zuò'ài 做爱 make love
zuǒbiān 左边 left-hand side
zuòcài 做菜 to cook
zuòchē 坐车 to ride (in car)
zuòchū nǔlì 做出努力 to make an effort
zuòde hǎo! 做得好 well done!
zuòfàn 做饭 cook, to
zuòguo 做过 to have done something
zuòhǎole 做好了 done (finished)
zuòjiā 作家 writer
zuòmèng 做梦 to dream
zuótiān 昨天 yesterday
zuówǎn 昨晚 last night
zuòwèi 座位 seat
zuòwén 作家 composition, writings
zuòxiàlai 坐下来 to sit down
zuǒyòu 左右 approximately
zúqiú 足球 soccer
zǔxiān 祖先 ancestor
zǔzhǐ 阻止 to prevent
zǔzhuāng 组装 to assemble, to put together

English–Chinese

A

abacus suànpán 算盘
abdomen fùbù 腹部
ability nénglì 能力
able to néng/kěyǐ 能 / 可以
able to understand (reading)
  kàndedǒng 看得懂
able to understand (hearing)
  tīngdedǒng 听得懂
about (approximately) dàyuē
  大约
about (regarding) yǒuguān
  有关
above shàngmiàn 上面
abroad guówài 国外
absent quēxí 缺席
accept, to jiēshòu 接受
accident shìgù 事故
accidentally, by chance
  ǒuránde 偶然地
accommodations zhùsù 住宿
accompany, to péi 陪
according to gēnjù 根据
accuse, to zhǐzé 指责
ache, to tòng 痛
acquaintance shúrén 熟人
acquainted, to be rènshi
  mǒurén 认识某人
across héngguò 横过
across from zài ... duìmiàn
  在 ... 对面
act, to zuò 做
action xíngdòng 行动
activity huódòng 活动
actually qíshí 其实
add, to jiā 加
address dìzhǐ 地址
admire, to qīnpèi 钦佩
admit, confess chéngrèn 承认
adult chéngrén 成人
advance, go forward qiánjìn
  前进

advance money, deposit
  yùfùkuǎn/yājīn
  预付款 / 押金
advice quàn'gào 劝告
advise, to chū zhǔyì 出主意
aeroplane fēijī 飞机
affect, to yǐngxiǎng 影响
affection gǎnqíng 感情
afford, to fùdāndeqǐ 负担得起
afraid pà 怕
after zài ... yǐhòu 在 ... 以后
afternoon (3 pm to dusk)
  xiàwǔ 下午
afternoon (midday) zhōngwǔ
  中午
afterwards, then hòulái 后来
again zài 再
age niánlíng 年龄
ago yǐqián 以前
agree, to tóngyì 同意
agreed! zànchéng 赞成
agreement xiédìng 协定
air kōngqì 空气
air conditioning kōngtiáo
  空调
airmail hángkōng yóujiàn
  航空邮件
airplane fēijī 飞机
airport fēijīchǎng 飞机场
a little yīdiǎnr 一点儿
a lot hěnduō 很多
alcohol, liquor jiǔ 酒
alike xiāngtóng 相同
alive huózhe 活着
all yīqiè 一切
alley, lane xiàng 巷
allow, permit yǔnxǔ 允许
allowed to róngxǔ 容许
almost jīhū 几乎
alone dāndú 单独
alphabet zìmǔ 字母
already yǐjīng 已经

45

A

also yě 也

altogether, in total yīgòng 一共

although suīrán 虽然

always zǒngshì 总是

ambassador dàshǐ 大使

America Měiguó 美国

American (in general) Měiguóde 美国的

American (people) Měiguórén 美国人

among zài ... zhī zhōng 在 ... 之中

amount shùliàng/shùmù 数量 / 数目

ancestor zǔxiān 祖先

ancient gǔdài 古代

and hé 和

anger fènnù 愤怒

angry shēngqì 生气

animal dòngwù 动物

ankle huái 踝

annoyed shēngqì 生气

another (different) bùtóngde 不同的

another (same again) zài yī (ge) 再一(个)

annual měi nián de 每年的

answer, to (spoken) huídá 回答

answer, to (written) dáfù 答复

answer the phone jiē diànhuà 接电话

answering machine liúyánjī 留言机

antiques gǔwán 古玩

anus gāngmén 肛门

anybody, anyone rènhé rén 任何人

anything rènhé shì 任何事

anywhere rènhé dìfang 任何地方

ape yuánrén 猿人

apart xiānggé 相隔

apart from chúle ... yǐwài 除了 ... 以外

apartment gōngyù 公寓

apologize, to dàoqiàn 道歉

apparently míngxiǎnde 明显地

appear, become visible chūxiàn 出现

appearance, looks yàngzi/wàimào 样子 / 外貌

apple píngguǒ 苹果

appliance, electrical diànqì 电器

apply, to (for permission) shēnqǐng 申请

appointment yuēhuì/yùyuē 约会 / 预约

approach, to (in space) jiējìn 接近

approach, to (in time) láilín 来临

appropriate shìdàngde 适当的

approximately dàyuē 大约

April Sìyuè 四月

architecture jiànzhù 建筑

area dìqū/fànwéi 地区 / 范围

argue, to zhēngchǎo 争吵

argument zhēnglùn/biànlùn 争论 / 辩论

arm gēbo 胳膊

armchair fúshǒuyǐ 扶手椅

army jūnduì/bùduì/lùjūn 军队 / 部队 / 陆军

around (approximately) dàyuē/zuǒyòu 大约 / 左右

around (nearby) fùjìn 附近

around (surrounding) zài ... zhōuwéi 在 ... 周围

arrange, to chóubàn 筹办

arrangements, planning ānpái 安排

arrival, to arrive dàodá 到达

art yìshù 艺术

article (in newspaper/journal) wénzhāng 文章

artificial réngōngde 人工的

artist yìshùjiā 艺术家

ashamed, embarrassed nánwéiqíng 难为情

Asia Yàzhōu 亚洲

ask about, to wèn 问

ask for, to yàoqiú 要求
asleep shuìzhe 睡着
assemble, gather jíhé 集合
assemble, put together
  zhuāngpèi/zǔzhuāng
  装配 / 组装
assistance, to assist
  bāngzhu/xiézhù 帮忙 / 协助
astonished chījīng/gǎndào
  jīngyà 吃惊 / 感到惊讶
as well yě 也
at zài 在
at home zài jiā 在家
at least qǐmǎ/zhìshǎo
  起码 / 至少
atmosphere, ambience qìfēn
  气氛
at night yèlǐ 夜里
at once mǎshàng/lìkè
  马上 / 立刻
attack (in war) gōngjī 攻击
attack (with words) píngjī
  评击
attain, reach dádào 达到
attempt qǐtú 企图
attempt, to chángshì 尝试
attend, to cānjiā 参加
at the latest zuìchí 最迟
attitude tàidu 态度
attract xīyǐn 吸引
attractive yǒu xīyǐnlì de/
  yòurén 有吸引力的 / 诱人
auction, to pāimài 拍卖
auctioned off pāimàidiào
  拍卖掉
August Bāyuè 八月
aunt (father's older/younger
  sister) gūmǔ, gūgu
  姑母 / 姑姑
aunt (wife of father's older
  brother) bómǔ 伯母
aunt (wife of father's younger
  brother) shūmǔ/shénmǔ
  叔母 / 婶母
aunt (wife of mother's older/
  younger brother) jiùmǔ 舅母
aunt (wife's mother's older/
  younger sister) yímǔ 姨母

Australia Àodàlìyà/Àozhōu
  澳大利亚 / 澳洲
Australian (in general)
  Àodàlìyàde/Àozhōude
  澳大利亚的 / 澳洲的
Australian (people)
  Àodàlìyàrén/Àozhōurén
  澳大利亚人 / 澳洲人
authority (person in charge)
  quánwēi 权威
authority (power) quánlì 权力
automobile, car qìchē 汽车
autumn qiūtiān 秋天
available kěhuòdéde 可获得的
available, to make kěyòngde
  可用的
average (numbers) píngjūn
  平均
average (so-so, just okay)
  yìbān 一般
awake xǐng 醒
awake, wake up xǐnglái 醒来
awaken, wake someone up
  jiàoxǐng 叫醒
aware yìshídào 意识到
awareness yìshí 意识

B

baby yīng'ér 婴儿
back (part of body) bèi 背
back, rear hòumiàn 后面
back, to go huíqù 回去
back up, to zhīchí 支持
backward luòhòu 落后
bad huài/zāo 坏 / 糟
bad luck dǎoméi 倒霉
bag dàizi 袋子
baggage xíngli 行李
bake, to kǎo 烤
bald guāngtūde 光秃的
ball qiú 球
ballpoint pen yuánzhūbǐ
  圆珠笔
banana xiāngjiāo 香蕉
bandage bēngdài 绷带
bank (finance) yínháng 银行

B

bank (of river) hé'àn 河岸
banquet yànhuì 宴会
bar (blocking way) páichì 排斥
bar (serving drinks) jiǔbā 酒吧
barber lǐfàdiàn 理发店
barely jǐnjǐn/jīhū méiyǒu
　仅仅 / 几乎没有
bargain, to jiǎngjià 讲价
barren pínjíde 贫瘠的
base, foundation jīchǔ 基础
based on gēnjù 根据
basic jīběn 基本
basis jīchǔ 基础
basket lánzi 篮子
basketball lánqiú 篮球
bathtub yùgāng, yùpén
　浴缸 / 浴盆
bathe, take a bath xǐzǎo 洗澡
bathe, swim yóuyǒng 游泳
bathrobe yùyī 浴衣
bathroom yùshì/xǐshǒujiān/
　cèsuǒ 浴室 / 洗手间 / 厕所
battle zhàndòu 战斗
bay hǎiwān 海湾
be, exist shì/yǒu 是 / 有
beach hǎitān 海滩
bean dòu 豆
beancurd dòufu 豆腐
beard húxū 胡须
beat (to defeat) dǎbài 打败
beat (to strike) qiāodǎ 敲打
beautiful (of people) měi/měilì
　美 / 美丽
beautiful (of places) yōuměi
　优美
beautiful (of things) hǎokàn
　好看
because yīnwèi 因为
become, to chéngwéi 成为
bed chuáng 床
bedding bèirù 被褥
bedclothes shuìyī 睡衣
bedroom wòshì 卧室
bedsheet chuángdān 床单
beef niúròu 牛肉
before (in front of) zài ...
　qiánmiàn 在 ... 前面
before (in time) yǐqián 以前

beforehand, earlier zhīqián
　之前
begin, to kāishǐ 开始
beginning kāitóu/kāiduān
　开头 / 开端
behave biǎoxiàn 表现
behind zài ... hòumiàn
　在 ... 后面
Beijing Běijīng 北京
belief, faith xìnyǎng 信仰
believe, to xiāngxìn 相信
belongings suǒyǒuwù/cáiwù
　所有物 / 财物
belong to shǔyú 属于
below xiàmiàn 下面
belt yāodài 腰带
beside zài ... pángbiān
　在 ... 旁边
besides chú cǐ zhīwài
　除此之外
best zuì hǎo 最好
best wishes zhù hǎo/
　liánghǎo zhùyuàn
　祝好 / 良好祝愿
better bǐjiào hǎo/gèng hǎo
　比较好 / 更好
better, get (be cured)
　hǎozhuǎn 好转
better, get (improve)
　jìnbùle hěnduō/biànhǎo
　进步了很多 / 变好
between zài ... zhījiān
　在 ... 之间
bicycle zìxíngchē 自行车
big dà 大
bill zhàngdān 帐单
billion shí yì 十亿
bird niǎo 鸟
birth, to give shēng 生
birthday shēngrì 生日
biscuit bǐnggān 饼干
bit (slightly) yīdiǎnr 一点儿
bite, to yǎo 咬
bitter kǔde 苦的
black hēisè 黑色
black beans dòuchǐ 豆豉
blame, to zéguài/guījiù
　责怪 / 归咎

bland dāndiào 单调
blanket tǎnzi 毯子
bleed, to liúxuè 流血
blood xuè 血
blood vessel xuèguǎn 血管
blouse nǚ chènshān 女衬衫
blue lánsè 蓝色
board, to (boat) shàngchuán
上船
board, to (bus, train) shàngchē
上车
boat chuán 船
body shēntǐ 身体
body weight tǐzhòng 体重
boil, to zhǔ 煮
boiled zhǔguode 煮过的
bone gǔtou 骨头
bon voyage! yī fān fēng shùn
一帆风顺
book shū 书
border (between countries)
biānjiè 边界
border, edge biānyuán 边缘
bored mèn/wúliáo 闷 / 无聊
boring méi yìsi 没意思
born, to be chūshēng 出生
borrow, to jiè 借
boss lǎobǎn 老板
botanic gardens zhíwùyuán
植物园
both liǎng ge 两个
both... and yòu ... yòu
又 ... 又
bother, disturb dǎrǎo/dǎjiǎo
打扰 / 打搅
bother, disturbance fánrǎo
烦扰
bottle píngzi 瓶子
bottom (base) dǐ 底
bottom (buttocks) pìgu 屁股
boundary, border biānjiè 边界
bowl wǎn 碗
box xiāng 箱
box (cardboard) hézi 盒子
boy nánháir 男孩儿
boyfriend nánpéngyou 男朋友
bra rǔzhào 乳罩
bracelet shǒuzhuó 手镯

brain nǎo 脑
brake, to brake shāchē/shāzhù
刹车 / 刹住
branch (company) fēnháng
分行
brand name míngpái 名牌
brave, daring yǒnggǎn 勇敢
bread miànbāo 面包
break, shatter nònghuài 弄坏
break apart, to zhéduàn 折断
break down, to (car, machine)
huàile 坏了
breakfast, morning meal
zǎofàn 早饭
breakfast, to eat chī zǎofàn
吃早饭
breasts rǔfáng 乳房
bride xīnniáng 新娘
bridegroom xīnláng 新郎
bridge qiáo 桥
brief jiǎnduǎn 简短
briefcase shǒutíbāo/
gōngwénbāo
手提包 / 公文包
briefs sānjiǎokù 三角裤
bright míngliàng 明亮
bring, to nálái 拿来
bring up (children) yǎngyù
养育
bring up, to (topic) tídào 提到
Britain Yīngguó 英国
British (in general) Yīngguóde
英国的
British (people) Yīngguórén
英国人
broad, spacious guǎngkuòde
广阔的
broadcast, program guǎngbō
广播
broadcast, to bōyīn 播音
broccoli xīlánhuācài 西兰花菜
broken, does not work, spoiled
huàile 坏了
broken, shattered dǎpòle
打破了
broken, snapped (of bones,
etc.) zhéduànle 折断了
broken off duànkāi 断开

B

bronze tóng/qīngtóng
铜 / 青铜
broom sàozhou 扫帚
broth, soup ròutāng 肉汤
brother (older) gēge 哥哥
brother (younger) dìdi 弟弟
brother-in-law (husband's
older brother) dàbó 大伯
brother-in-law (husband's
younger brother) xiǎoshū
小叔
brother-in-law (wife's older
brother) nèixiōng 内兄
brother-in-law (wife's older
sister's husband) jiěfu 姐夫
brother-in-law (wife's younger
brother) nèidì 内弟
brother-in-law (wife's younger
sister's husband) mèifu 妹夫
brown hèsè/zōngsè
褐色 / 棕色
bruise qīngzhǒng 青肿
brush shuāzi 刷子
brush, to shuā 刷
bucket shuǐtǒng 水桶
Buddhism Fójiào 佛教
Buddhist (in general) Fójiàode
佛教的
Buddhist (people) Fójiàotú
佛教徒
buffalo (water buffalo) shuǐniú
水牛
build, to gài/jiàn 盖 / 建
building dàlóu 大楼
burn (injury) shāoshāng 烧伤
burn, to shāo 烧
burned down, out bèi shāohuǐ/
shāotā 被烧毁 / 烧塌
Burma Miǎndiàn 缅甸
Burmese (in general)
Miǎndiànde 缅甸的
Burmese (people)
Miǎndiànrén 缅甸人
bus gōnggòngqìchē 公共汽车
bus station qìchēzhàn 汽车站
business shāngyè 商业
businessperson shāngrén
商人

busy (doing something)
máng 忙
busy (crowded) yōngjǐ 拥挤
busy (telephone) zhànxiàn
占线
but dànshì 但是
butter huángyóu 黄油
butterfly húdié 蝴蝶
buttocks pìgu 屁股
buy, to mǎi 买
by means of yòng 用
by the way shùnbiàn wèn
yīxià 顺便问一下

C

cabbage juǎnxīncài 卷心菜
cabbage, Chinese báicài 白菜
cake, pastry dàn'gāo 蛋糕
calculate jìsuàn/hésuàn
计算 / 核算
calculator jìsuànjī 计算机
call, summon zhàojiàn/
chuánxùn 召见 / 传讯
call on the telephone
dǎ diànhuà 打电话
called, named míng jiào 名叫
calm píngjìng 平静
Cambodia Gāomián/
Jiǎnpǔzhài 高棉 / 柬埔寨
Cambodian (in general)
Gāomiánde/Jiǎnpǔzhàide
高棉的 / 柬埔寨的
Cambodian (people)
Gāomiánrén/Jiǎnpǔzhàirén
高棉人 / 柬埔寨人
camera zhàoxiàngjī 照相机
can, be able to kěyǐ 可以
can, may néng 能
can, tin guàntóu 罐头
cancel qǔxiāo 取消
candle làzhú 蜡烛
candy, sweets tángguǒ
糖果
can't see kànbujiàn 看不见
can't see clearly
kànbuqīngchu 看不清楚

Cantonese (in general)
Guǎngzhōude 广州的
Cantonese (language)
Guǎngzhōuhuà 广州话
Cantonese (people)
Guǎngzhōurén 广州人
capable of, to be yǒu nénglì
有能力
capture, to bǔhuò 捕获
car, automobile qìchē 汽车
cardboard yìngzhǐbǎn 硬纸版
cards, game pùkèpái 扑克牌
care for, love àihù 爱护
care of, to take zhàogu 照顾
careful! xiǎoxīn 小心
carpet dìtǎn 地毯
carrot húluóbo 胡萝卜
carry, to tí/dài/zài 提／带／载
cart (horsecart) mǎchē 马车
cart (pushcart) shǒutuīchē
手推车
carve, to diāokè 雕刻
carving diāokèpǐn 雕刻品
cash, money xiànkuǎn 现款
cash a check, to duìxiàn 兑现
cassette héshì cídài 盒式磁带
cat māo 猫
catch, to zhuāzhù 抓住
Catholic (religion) Tiānzhǔjiào
天主教
Catholic (in general)
Tiānzhǔjiàode 天主教的
Catholic (people)
Tiānzhǔjiàotú 天主教徒
cauliflower huācài 花菜
cause yuányīn 原因
cautious xiǎoxīnde 小心的
cave yándòng 岩洞
CD guāngpán/guāngdié
光盘／光碟
CD-ROM guāngpán yuèdúqì
光盘阅读器
ceiling tiānhuābǎn 天花板
celebrate, to qìngzhù 庆祝
celery qíncài 芹菜
center (of city) (shì) zhōngxīn
(市) 中心
center, middle zhōngjiān 中间

central zhōngyāng 中央
century shìjì 世纪
ceremony diǎnlǐ 典礼
certain, sure yīdìng 一定
certainly! dāngrán kěyǐ
当然可以
certificate zhèngshū 证书
chair yǐzi 椅子
challenge tiǎozhàn 挑战
champion guànjūn 冠军
chance, by ǒurán 偶然
chance, opportunity jīhuì
机会
change, exchange (money)
duìhuàn 兑换
change, small língqián 零钱
change, switch (clothes)
huàn 换
change, to (bus/train)
zhuǎnchē 转车
change, to (conditions,
situations) gǎibiàn 改变
change one's mind gǎibiàn
zhǔyì 改变主意
character (Chinese) Hànzì
汉字
character (personality) xìnggé
性格
characteristic tèdiǎn 特点
chase, to zhuī 追
chase away, chase out
gǎnchū 赶出
cheap piányi 便宜
cheat, someone who cheats
piànzi 骗子
cheat, to piàn 骗
check, verify jiǎnchá 检查
checked (pattern) fānggéde
方格的
cheek miànjiá 面颊
cheers! gānbēi 干杯
cheese nǎilào/rǔlào
奶酪／乳酪
chess guójì xiàngqí 国际象棋
chest (box) xiāngzi 箱子
chest (breast) xiōngqiāng
胸腔
chew, to jué/jǔjué 嚼／咀嚼

chicken jī 鸡
child (offspring) háizi 孩子
child (young person) xiǎohái
小孩
chilli pepper làjiāo 辣椒
chilli sauce làjiāojiàng 辣椒酱
chilled bīngzhèn 冰镇
chin xiàba 下巴
China Zhōngguó 中国
Chinese (in general)
Zhōngguóde 中国的
Chinese (language) Zhōngwén/
Hànyǔ 中文／汉语
Chinese (people) Zhōngguórén
中国人
Chinese chess Zhōngguó
xiàngqí 中国象棋
chocolate qiǎokèlì 巧克力
choice xuǎnzé 选择
choose, to xuǎnzé 选择
chopsticks kuàizi 筷子
Christian (in general)
Jīdùtújiàode 基督教的
Christian (people) Jīdùtú
基督徒
Christianity Jīdùjiào 基督教
church jiàotáng 教堂
cigar xuějiāyān 雪茄烟
cigarette xiāngyān 香烟
cinema diànyǐngyuàn 电影院
circle yuánquān 圆圈
circle (theater) lóutīng 楼厅
citizen shìmín/gōngmín
市民／公民
citrus gānjúshǔde 柑橘属的
city chéngshì 城市
class, category zhǒnglèi 种类
classes (at university) kè 课
clean gānjìng 干净
clean, to nòng gānjìng 弄干净
cleanliness qīngjié 清洁
clear (of weather) fàngqíngle
放晴了
clever cōngmíng 聪明
climate qìhòu 气候
climb onto páshàng 爬上
climb up (hills, mountains)
pāndēng 攀登

clock shízhōng/zhōng
时钟／钟
close, to cover héqǐ 合起
close to, nearby jìn/kàojìn
近／靠近
close together, tight kàojǐn
靠紧
closed (door/shop) guānmén/
guānshàngle 关门／关上了
closed (road) fēngsuǒ 封锁
cloth bù 布
clothes, clothing yīfu 衣服
cloudy, overcast duōyún 多云
cloves bàn 瓣
co-worker, colleague tóngshì
同事
coat, jacket wàiyī 外衣
coat, overcoat dàyī 大衣
coconut yēzi 椰子
coffee kāfēi 咖啡
coin yìngbì 硬币
cold lěng 冷
cold, flu gǎnmào 感冒
colleague, co-worker tóngshì
同事
collect payment, to shōukuǎn
收款
collide, to xiāngzhuàng 相撞
collision zhuàngchē 撞车
color yánsè 颜色
comb shūzi 梳子
combine sounds into syllables
pīnyīn 拼音
come, to lái 来
come back huílai 回来
come in jìnlái 进来
come on, let's go kuài! 快！
comfortable shūfu 舒服
command, order mìnglìng
命令
command, to zhǐhuī 指挥
common, frequent pǔtōngde
普通的
company, firm gōngsī 公司
compare, to bǐjiào 比较
compared with yǔ ... xiāngbǐ
与 ... 相比
compete, to jìngzhēng 竞争

competition bǐsài 比赛

complain, to bàoyuàn 抱怨

complaint tóusù 投诉

complete (finished) jiéshù 结束

complete (thorough) chèdǐ
彻底

complete (whole) quánbù 全部

complete, to wánchéng 完成

completely wánquán/chèdǐ
完全 / 彻底

complicated fùzá 复杂

composition, writings
zuòwén/xiězuò 作文 / 写作

compulsory qiángzhìxìngde/
guīdìngde 强制性的 / 规定的

computer diànnǎo/jìsuànjī
电脑 / 计算机

computer (main) zhǔjī 主机

comrade tóngzhì 同志

concentrate, to jízhōng 集中

concerning yǒuguān/guānyú
有关 / 关于

concert yīnyuèhuì 音乐会

concert hall yīnyuètīng 音乐厅

condensed milk liànrǔ 炼乳

condition (pre-condition)
xiānjué tiáojiàn 先决条件

condition (status) zhuàngtài/
qíngkuàng 状态 / 情况

condition (subjective/objective)
tiáojiàn 条件

condom bìyùntào 避孕套

confectionery tángguǒ 糖果

confidence xìnxīn 信心

confidence, to have yǒu
xìnxīn 有信心

confirm quèrèn 确认

Confucianism Rújiāsīxiǎng/
Rújiào 儒家思想 / 儒教

confuse, to hùnxiáo 混淆

confused (in a mess) hùnluàn
混乱

confused (mentally) hútu 糊涂

confusing shǐ hùnluàn 使混乱

congratulations! zhùhè nǐ
祝贺你

connect together, to liánjiē
连接

connection (transport)
liánjiēdiǎn/zhōngzhuǎnzhàn
连接点 / 中转站

conscious of, to be yìshídào
意识到

consider (to have an opinion)
rènwéi 认为

consider (to think over) kǎolǜ
考虑

constipation biànmì 便秘

consulate lǐngshìguǎn 领事馆

consult, talk over with
gēn ... shāngliang 跟 ... 商量

consultation (by doctor)
kànbìng/jiùzhěn 看病 / 就诊

contact, connection liánxì
联系

contact, get in touch with
gēn ... liánxì 跟 ... 联系

contact lens yǐnxíng yǎnjìng
隐型眼镜

contagious chuánrǎnde
传染的

continent zhōu/dàlù 洲 / 大陆

continue, to jìxù 继续

contraceptive bìyùn 避孕

contraceptive pill bìyùnyào
避孕药

contract hétóng/qìyuē
合同 / 契约

convenient fāngbiàn 方便

conversation huìhuà 会话

cook (person) chúshī 厨师

cook (verb) zuòcài 做菜

cook, to zuòfàn 做饭

cooked zhǔshóude 煮熟的

cooker, stove lúzi 炉子

cookie, sweet biscuit
xiǎotiánbǐng 小甜饼

cooking, cuisine fēngwèi
fàncài/pēngtiáo 风味饭菜 /
烹调

cool liángkuài 凉快

cool, to shǐ lěngquè 使冷却

copper tóng/zǐtóng 铜 / 紫铜

copy fùběn 副本

copy (verb) chāoxiě/mófǎng
抄写 / 模仿

coral shānhú 珊瑚
corn, grain yùmǐ 玉米
corner jiǎoluò 角落
correct duì/zhèngquè
    对 / 正确
correct, to jiǎozhèng/gǎizhèng
    矫正 / 改正
correspond (write letters)
    tōngxìn 通信
corridor zǒuláng 走廊
corrupt fǔbài 腐败
cosmetics huàzhuāngpǐn
    化妆品
cost chéngběn 成本
cost (expense) fèiyòng 费用
cost (price) jiàgé 价格
costly guì/ángguì 贵 / 昂贵
costume mínzú fúzhuāng/
    xìzhuāng 民族服装 / 戏装
cot yīng'érchuáng/
    tóngchuáng 婴儿床 / 童床
cotton miánbù 棉布
cotton wool miánhuā 棉花
couch, sofa shāfā 沙发
cough késoushēng 咳嗽声
cough, to késou 咳嗽
cough lolly rùnhóutáng 润喉糖
cough syrup késou yàoshuǐ
    咳嗽药水
could, might kěnéng 可能
count shǔ/suàn 数 / 算
count, reckon rènwéi 认为
counter (for paying, buying
    tickets) guìtái 柜台
country (rural area) xiāngxià
    乡下
country (nation) guójiā 国家
courtyard yuànzi 院子
courtesy lǐmào 礼貌
cover, to gài 盖
cow mǔniú 母牛
crab pángxiè 螃蟹
cracked lièkāile 裂开了
cracker, salty biscuit xián
    bǐnggān 咸饼干
crafts shǒugōngyì 手工艺
craftsperson gōngjiàng/
    shǒuyìrén 工匠 / 手艺人

crashed (car) zhuàngchē 撞车
crashed (computer) sǐjī 死机
crazy fēngkuángde 疯狂的
create, to chuàngzuò/
    chuàngzào 创作 / 创造
credit card xìnyòngkǎ 信用卡
criminal zuìfàn 罪犯
cross, angry shēngqì 生气
cross, go over yuèguò 越过
crossroads shízìlùkǒu
    十字路口
crowded yōngjǐ 拥挤
cruel cánrěn 残忍
cry jiàohǎn 叫喊
cry, to kū 哭
cry out, to hǎn 喊
cucumber huángguā 黄瓜
cuisine, style of cooking
    fēngwèicài 风味菜
culture wénhuà 文化
cup bēizi 杯子
cupboard guìzi 柜子
cure (medical) zhìliáo 治疗
cured, preserved bèi jiāgōng
    chùlǐ 被加工处理
currency qiánbì 钱币
curtain chuānglián 窗帘
custom, tradition xísú 习俗
cut (injury) shāngkǒu 伤口
cut, to gē 割
cute, appealing kě'ài 可爱

D

daily rìchángde 日常的
damage pòhuài 破坏
damage, to sǔnhuài 损坏
damp cháoshī 潮湿
dance wǔhuì 舞会
dance, to tiàowǔ 跳舞
danger wēixiǎn 危险
dangerous wēixiǎnde 危险的
dark àn/hēi'àn 暗 / 黑暗
date (of the month) rìqī 日期
date of birth chūshēng rìqī
    出生日期
daughter nǚ'ér 女儿

daughter-in-law xífù 媳妇
dawn límíng 黎明
day tiān 天
day after tomorrow hòutiān
后天
day before yesterday qiántiān
前天
day of the week gōngzuòrì
工作日
day off xiūjiàtiān 休假天
daydream, to zuò báirìmèng
做白日梦
dead sǐle 死了
deaf lóngde 聋的
death sǐwáng 死亡
debt zhài 债
deceive, to qīpiàn 欺骗
December Shí'èryuè 十二月
decide, to juédìng 决定
decision juédìng 决定
decline (get less) jiǎnruò/
jiǎnshǎo/xiàjiàng
减弱／减少／下降
decline (refuse) jùjué 拒绝
decorate, to zhuāngshì 装饰
decrease, to jiǎnshǎo 减少
deep shēn 深
defeat, to dǎbài 打败
defecate, to dàbià/jiě dàbiàn
大便／解大便
defect quēdiǎn 缺点
defend (in war) bǎowèi 保卫
defend (with words) biànhù
辩护
definite míngquède 明确的
degree, level chéngdù 程度
degrees (temperature) dù 度
delay, to dān'ge 耽搁
delayed (train, bus etc.)
wǎndiǎn 晚点
delicious hǎochī/shuǎngkǒu
好吃／爽口
deliver, to yùnsòng 运送
demand, to yāoqiú 要求
depart, to líkāi 离开
department bùmén 部门
department store
bǎihuò shāngdiàn 百货商店

departure chūfā 出发
depend on, to yīkào 依靠
deposit (leave behind with
someone) cúnfàng 存放
deposit (put money in the bank)
cúnkuǎn 存款
descendant hòuyì 后裔
describe, to miáoshù 描述
desert (arid land) shāmò 沙漠
desert, to abandon pāoqì 抛弃
desire yuànwàng 愿望
desire, to xiǎng 想
desk shūzhuō 书桌
dessert tiánshí 甜食
destination mùdìdì 目的地
destroy, to pòhuài 破坏
destroyed, ruined cuīhuǐ 摧毁
detergent qùgòujì 去垢剂
determined, stubborn jiānjué
坚决
develop, to (film) chōngxǐ
冲洗
develop, to (happen) kāizhǎn
开展
development fāzhǎn 发展
diagonal duìjiǎoxiàn 对角线
diagonally duìjiǎode 对角地
dial, to (telephone) bō diànhuà
拨电话
dialect fāngyán 方言
diamond zuànshí 钻石
diary rìjì 日记
dictionary cídiǎn/zìdiǎn
词典／字典
die, to sǐ 死
difference (discrepancy in
figures) chābié 差别
difference (in quality) chāyì
差异
different, other bùtóng 不同
difficult kùnnan 困难
dinner, evening meal wǎnfàn
晚饭
dinner, to eat chī wǎnfàn
吃晚饭
direction fāngxiàng 方向
director (of company)
dǒngshìzhǎng 董事长

D

dirt, filth wūgòu 污垢
dirty zāng 脏
disappointed shīwàng 失望
disaster zāinàn 灾难
discount yōuhuì 优惠
discover, to fāxiàn 发现
discussion, to discuss tǎolùn
  讨论
disease jíbìng 疾病
diesel oil cháiyóu 柴油
disgusting yànwùde 厌恶的
dish, platter pánzi 盘子
dish (particular food) fàncài
  饭菜
diskette cípán 磁盘
dislike, to yànwù 厌恶
display zhǎnlǎn 展览
display, to chénliè 陈列
dispute jiūfēn 纠纷
distance jùlí 距离
disturb, to dǎrǎo/dǎjiǎo
  打扰 / 打搅
disturbance sāoluàn 骚乱
divide, split up fēnkāi 分开
divided by chú yú 除于
divorce, to líhūn 离婚
divorced lílehūn 离了婚
do, perform an action zuò 做
do one's best jìn suǒ néng
  尽所能
doctor yīshēng/dàifu
  医生 / 大夫
document, letter wénjiàn 文件
dog gǒu 狗
done (cooked) zhǔshóule
  煮熟了
done (finished) zuòhǎole
  做好了
don't! búyào 不要
don't mention it! bú kèqi
  不客气
door mén 门
double shuāngbèi 双倍
doubt, to huáiyí 怀疑
down, downward xiàng xià
  向下
downstairs lóuxià 楼下
downtown shìzhōngxīn 市中心

dozen yī dá 一打
draw, to huà 画
drawer chōutī 抽屉
drawing tú 图
dream mèng 梦
dream, to zuòmèng 做梦
dress, frock liányīqún 连衣裙
dressed, to get chuānbàn
  穿扮
dressing gown chényī 晨衣
drink, refreshment yǐnliào
  饮料
drink, to hē 喝
drive, to (a car) kāichē 开车
drought hànzāi 旱灾
drown, to yānnì/yānsǐ
  淹溺 / 淹死
drug (medicine) yào 药
drug (recreational) dúpǐn 毒品
drugstore, pharmacy
  yàofáng 药房
drunk hēzuì 喝醉
dry gān 干
dry (weather) gānzào 干燥
dry, to nònggān 弄干
dry out (in the sun) liànggān
  晾干
duck yāzi 鸭子
dull (boring) mèn 闷
dull (weather) yīn'àn 阴暗
dumpling jiǎozi 饺子
during zài ... qījiān 在 ... 期间
dusk huánghūn 黄昏
dust huīchén 灰尘
duty (import tax) guānshuì
  关税
duty (responsibility) zérèn
  责任
DVD shùjù lùxiàngjī
  数据录象机

E

each, every měi 每
ear ěrduo 耳朵
earlier, beforehand shìxiān
  事先

early zǎo 早
early in the morning qīngzǎo 清早
earn, to zhèng/zhuàn 挣 / 赚
earrings ěrhuán 耳环
earth, soil nítǔ 泥土
Earth, the world dìqiú 地球
earthquake dìzhèn 地震
east dōngbiān 东边
easy róngyì 容易
eat, to chī 吃
economical shíhuì 实惠
economy jīngjì 经济
edge biānyuán 边缘
educate, to jiàoyù 教育
education jiàoyù 教育
effect, result xiàoguǒ 效果
effort nǔlì 努力
effort, to make an zuòchū nǔlì 做出努力
egg jīdàn 鸡蛋
eggplant, aubergine qiézi 茄子
eight bā 八
eighteen shíbā 十八
eighty bāshí 八十
either rènhé yī ge 任何一个
elbow zhǒu 肘
elder zhǎngbèi 长辈
election xuǎnjǔ 选举
electric diàndòngde 电动的
electricity diànliú 电流
electronic diànzi 电子
elegant yǎzhìde/gāoyǎ 雅致的 / 高雅
elephant dàxiàng 大象
elevator diàntī 电梯
eleven shíyī 十一
else: anything else biéde 别的
else: or else (yào) bùrán/fǒuzé (要) 不然 / 否则
email (message) diànzi yóujiàn/yīmèir 电子邮件 / 依妹儿
email, to fā diànzi yóujiàn/fā yīmèir 发电子邮件 / 发依妹儿
email address diànzi yóujiàn dìzhǐ 电子邮件地址

embarrassed nánwéiqíng 难为情
embarrassing shǐ rén nánkān 使人难堪
embassy dàshǐguǎn 大使馆
embrace, to yōngbào 拥抱
embroidered xiùhuāde 绣花的
embroidery cìxiù 刺绣
emergency jízhěn 急诊
emotion gǎnqíng/qíngxù 感情 / 情绪
empty kōngde 空的
end (finish) zhōngzhǐ 终止
end (tip) jiānduān/dǐngduān 尖端 / 顶端
end, to jiéshù 结束
enemy dírén 敌人
energy jīnglì 精力
engaged (telephone) zhànxiàn 占线
engaged (to be married) dìnghūn 订婚
engine fādòngjī 发动机
England Yīngguó 英国
English (in general) Yīngguóde 英国的
English (language) Yīngwén/Yīngyǔ 英文 / 英语
English (people) Yīngguórén 英国人
engrave, to kèshàng/diāo 刻上 / 雕
enjoy, to xiǎngshòu 享受
enjoy oneself, to guòde kuàihuó 过得快活
enjoyable yúkuàide 愉快的
enlarge, to kuòdà 扩大
enough zúgòu 足够
enquire, to wèn 问
enter, to jìnrù 进入
entire quánbù 全部
entirety, whole quánbùde 全部的
entrance, way in rùkǒu 入口
envelope xìnfēng 信封
envious yǐnqǐ xiànmù de 引起羡慕的

E

environment, the huánjìng
环境

envy xiànmù 羡慕

equal píngděngde 平等的

equality píngděng 平等

error cuòwù 错误

escalator diàndòng lóutī
电动楼梯

especially yóuqíshì 尤其是

establish, set up jiànlì 建立

Europe Ōuzhōu 欧洲

even (also) lián 连

even (smooth) pínghuá
平滑

evening wǎnshang 晚上

event shìjiàn 事件

ever, have already céng 曾

every měi 每

every kind of gèshì-gèyàng
各式各样

every time měi cì 每次

everybody, everyone
měi ge rén 每个人

everything měi jiàn shì/yīqiè
每件事 / 一切

everywhere měi ge dìfang/
dàochù 每个地方 / 到处

exact, exactly jīngquède/
quèqiè 精确的 / 确切

exactly! just so! yīdiǎn búcuò
一点不错

exam, test kǎoshì 考试

examine, to jiǎnchá 检查

example lìzi 例子

example, for bǐrú 比如

excellent yōuxiù de 优秀的

except chú ... zhīwài
除 ... 之外

exchange, to (money, opinions)
duìhuàn 兑换

exchange rate duìhuànlǜ
兑换率

excited gǎndào xīngfèn
感到兴奋

exciting lìng rén xīngfèn de
令人兴奋的

excuse me! (apology) duìbuqǐ
对不起

excuse me! (attracting
attention) qǐngwèn 请问

excuse me! (getting past)
láojià 劳驾

exist, to cúnzài 存在

exit, way out chūkǒu 出口

expand, grow larger
péngzhàng 膨胀

expect, to qīwàng 期望

expenses fèiyòng 费用

expensive guì 贵

experience jīngyàn 经验

experience, to tǐyàn/jīnglì
体验 / 经历

expert zhuānjiā 专家

explain, to jiěshì 解释

export, to export chūkǒu 出口

express, state biǎoshì 表示

extension (telephone) fēnjī
分机

extra éwàide 额外的

extremely jídùde 极度地

eye yǎnjing 眼睛

eyebrow yǎnméi 眼眉

eyeglasses, spectacles
yǎnjìng 眼镜

F

fabric, textile bùliào 布料

face liǎn 脸

face, to miànduì 面对

fact shìshí 是实

factory gōngchǎng 工厂

fail, to bù jígé/shībài
不及格 / 失败

failure shībài 失败

fall (season) qiūtiān 秋天

fall, to luòxià/diàoxià
落下 / 掉下

fall over shuāidǎo/dǎoxiàlái
摔倒 / 倒下来

false (imitation) màopáihuò/
jiǎmàode 冒牌货 / 假冒的

false (not true) jiǎde 假的

family jiātíng 家庭

famine jīhuāng 饥荒

famous yǒumíng/chúmíng 有名／出名
fan (admirer) mí, kuángrè àihàozhě 迷，狂热爱好者
fan (electrical) diànfēngshàn 电风扇
fan (for cooling) shànzi 扇子
fancy qítède 奇特的
far yuǎn 远
fare piàojià 票价
fast, rapid kuài 快
fast, to shǒuzhāi/zhāijiè 守斋／斋戒
fat, grease yóunì 油腻
fat, plump pàng 胖
father fùqin/bàba 父亲／爸爸
father-in-law (wife's father) yuèfù 岳父
fault guòcuò 过错
fax (machine) chuánzhēnjī 传真机
fax (message) chuánzhēn 传真
fax, to fā chuánzhēn 发传真
fear kǒngjù 恐惧
February èryuè 二月
fee shōufèi 收费
feed, to wèi 喂
feel, to juéde 觉得
feeling gǎnjué 感觉
female nǚde/cíde 女的／雌的
fence líbā/shānlán 篱笆／栅栏
ferry dùchuán 渡船
fertile féiwòde 肥沃的
festival jiérì 节日
fetch, to qǔ 取
fever fāshāo 发烧
few jíshǎo/jǐge 极少／几个
fiancé wèihūnfū 未婚夫
fiancée wèihūnqī 未婚妻
field, empty space kōngdì 空地
fierce xiōngměngde 凶猛的
fifteen shíwǔ 十五
fifty wǔshí 五十
fight, to (physically) dǎjià 打架
fight over, to zhēng 争

figure, number shùzi 数字
Filipino (in general) Fēilǜbīnde 菲律宾的
Filipino (language) Fēilǜbīnyǔ 菲律宾语
Filipino (people) Fēilǜbīnrén 菲律宾人
Filipino (Tagalog) Fēilǜbīnyǔ 菲律宾语
fill, to zhuāngmǎn 装满
fill out (form) tiánbiǎo 填表
film (camera) jiāojuǎn 胶卷
film, movie diànyǐng 电影
final zuìhòu 最后
finally zhōngyú 终于
find, to zhǎo 找
fine (okay) hǎo 好
fine (punishment) fákuǎn 罚款
finger shǒuzhǐ 手指
finish wánchéng 完成
finish off, to jiéshù 结束
finished (completed) wánjiéle 完结了
finished (none left) yòngguāngle 用光了
fire huǒ 火
fire someone, to jiěgù 解雇
fireworks yānhuā 烟花
firm (definite) jiāndìng 坚定
firm (mattress) jiānshíde 坚实的
firm, company shānghángl/gōngsī 商行／公司
first, earlier, beforehand xiān 先
fish yú 鱼
fish, to diàoyú 钓鱼
fish sauce yúlù 鱼露
fit, to (shǐ) shìhé (使) 适合
fitness training jiànshēn duànliàn 健身锻炼
fitting, suitable shìhéde 适合的
fitting room shìyīshì 试衣室
five wǔ 五
fix, to (a time, appointment) yuēdìng 约定
fix, to (repair) xiūlǐ 修理
flag qí 旗

F

flash (camera) shǎnguāngdēng 闪光灯

flashlight, torch shǒudiàntǒng 手电筒

flavor wèidào 味道

flat, apartment gōngyù 公寓

flat, smooth píngtǎnde 平坦的

flight bānjī 班机

flight number bānjīhào 班机号

flood hóngshuǐ 洪水

floor lóu/céng 楼／层

flour miànfěn 面粉

flower huā 花

flush (wash) chōngxǐ 冲洗

fly (insect) cāngyíng 苍蝇

fly, to fēi 飞

flu gǎnmào 感冒

fluent liúlì 流利

flute chángdí 长笛

fog wù 雾

fold, to zhédié 折叠

follow along, to yánzhe 沿着

follow behind, to gēnzhe 跟着

following gēnsuí/yǐxià 跟随／以下

fond of, to be xǐ'ài 喜爱

food shíwù 食物

foot jiǎo 脚

for wèi 为

for ever yǒngyuǎn 永远

forbid, to bùxǔ 不许

forbidden bèi jìnzhǐ de 被禁止的

force lìliang 力量

force, compel qiángpò 强迫

forehead é 额

foreign wàiguóde 外国的

foreigner wàiguórén 外国人

forest sēnlín 森林

forget, to wàngjì 忘记

forget about, to hūlüè 忽略

forgive, to yuánliàng 原谅

forgiveness, mercy kuānshù 宽恕

forgotten wàngle 忘了

fork chāzi 叉子

form (to fill out) biǎogé 表格

formalities shǒuxù 手续

fortress bǎolěi 堡垒

fortunately xìngyùnde 幸运地

forty sìshí 四十

forward xiàng qián 向前

four sì 四

fourteen shísì 十四

France Fǎguó 法国

free of charge miǎnfèi 免费

free of restraints wúxiànzhì 无限制

freedom zìyóu 自由

freeze jiébīng 结冰

French (in general) Fǎguóde 法国的

French (language) Fǎyǔ/Fǎwén 法语／法文

French (people) Fǎguórén 法国人

free, independent zìyóude 自由的

frequent jīngcháng 经常

fresh xīnxiān 新鲜

Friday Xīngqīwǔ/Lǐbàiwǔ 星期五／礼拜五

fried yóuzhá 油炸

friend péngyou 朋友

friendly yǒuhǎo 友好

frightened bèi xiàzhe 被吓着

from cóng 从

front qiánmiàn 前面

front: in front of zài ... de qiánmiàn 在 ... 的前面

frown zhòuméi 皱眉

frown, to duì ... zhòu méitou 对 ... 皱眉头

freeze (computer) sǐjī 死机

frozen bīngdòng 冰冻

fruit shuǐguǒ 水果

fry, to jiān 煎

fulfill lǚxíng 履行

full mǎn 满

full, eaten one's fill chībǎo 吃饱

fun, to have wánr 玩儿

function, to work qǐ zuòyòng 起作用

funds, funding jīngfèi 经费

funeral zànglǐ 葬礼

fungus zhēnjūn 真菌
funny hǎoxiào 好笑
furniture jiājù 家具
further, additional jìnyībùde
　进一步的
fussy dàjīngxiǎoguàide
　大惊小怪的
future: in future jiānglái 将来

G

gamble dǔbó 赌博
game yóuxì 游戏
garage (for parking)
　chēfáng/chēkù 车房 / 车库
garage (for repairs)
　xiūchēháng 修车行
garbage lājī 拉圾
garden, yard huāyuán 花园
gardens, park gōngyuán 公园
garlic dàsuàn 大蒜
garment yīfu 衣服
gasoline qìyóu 汽油
gasoline station jiāyóuzhàn
　加油站
gate (main entrance) dàmén
　大门
gather, to shōují 收集
gender xìngbié 性别
general, all-purpose
　quánmiànde 全面的
generally pǔbiànde 普遍地
generous kāngkǎide 慷慨
gentle wényǎde 文雅的
German (in general) Déguóde
　德国的
German (language) Déyǔ/
　Déwén 德语 / 德文
German (people) Déguórén
　德国人
Germany Déguó 德国
gesture zīshì 姿势
get, receive dédào 得到
get off (boat) xiàchuán 下船
get off (bus/train) xiàchē 下车
get on (boat) shàngchuán
　上船

get on (bus/train) shàngchē
　上车
get up (from bed) qǐchuáng
　起床
get well soon! zǎorì kāngfú
　早日康复
ghost guǐ 鬼
gift lǐwù 礼物
ginger jiāng 姜
girl nǚháir/gūniang
　女孩儿 / 姑娘
girlfriend nǚpéngyou 女朋友
give, to gěi 给
given name míngzi 名字
glad gāoxìng 高兴
glass (for drinking) bēizi 杯子
glass (material) bōli 玻璃
glasses, spectacles yǎnjìng
　眼镜
glutinous rice nuòmǐ 糯米
go, to qù 去
go along, join in cānyǔ 参与
go around, visit cānguān 参观
go back huíqù 回去
go beyond chāochū 超出
go for a walk chūqù zǒuzou
　出去走走
go home huíjiā 回家
go out (fire, candle) xīmiè 熄灭
go out, exit chūqù 出去
go to bed shuìjiào 睡觉
go up, climb dēngshàng 登上
goal mùdì 目的
goat shānyáng 山羊
God Shàngdì 上帝
god shén 神
goddess nǚshén 女神
gold jīn 金
golf gāo'ěrfūqiú 高尔夫球
gone, finished bújiànle 不见了
good hǎo 好
good luck! zhù nǐ hǎoyùn
　祝你好运
goodbye zàijiàn 再见
goodness! wǒde tiān 我的天
goose é 鹅
government zhèngfǔ 政府
gradually zhújiànde 逐渐地

G

grand, great wěidàde 伟大的

granddaughter (maternal)
wàisūnnǚ 外孙女

granddaughter (paternal)
sūnnǚ 孙女

grandfather (maternal)
wàizǔfù/lǎoye 外祖父 / 姥爷

grandfather (paternal)
zǔfù/yéye 祖父 / 爷爷

grandmother (maternal)
wàizǔmǔ/lǎolao
外祖母 / 姥姥

grandmother (paternal)
zǔmǔ/nǎinai 祖母 / 奶奶

grandparents (maternal)
wàizǔfùmǔ 外祖父母

grandparents (paternal)
zǔfùmǔ 祖父母

grandson (maternal)
wàisūnzi 外孙子

grandson (paternal) sūnzi
孙子

grapes pútao 葡萄

grass cǎo 草

grateful gǎnjī 感激

grave fénmù 坟墓

great, impressive wěidà 伟大

green lǜsè 绿色

greens shūcài 蔬菜

greet, to huānyíng 欢迎

greetings wènhòu 问候

grey huīsè 灰色

grill, to shāokǎo 烧烤

ground, earth dìmiàn 地面

group tuántǐ 团体

grow, be growing (plant)
zhǎng 长

grow, cultivate zhòngzhí 种植

grow larger, to zēngzhǎng
增长

grow up (child) zhǎngdà 长大

Guangzhou (Canton)
Guǎngzhōu 广州

guarantee bǎozhèng 保证

guarantee, to dānbǎo 担保

guard, to bǎohù 保护

guess, to cāi 猜

guest kèren 客人

guest of honor guìbīn 贵宾

guesthouse bīnguǎn 宾馆

guide, lead dǎoyóu 导游

guidebook lǚyóu zhǐnán
旅游指南

guilty (of a crime) yǒuzuì 有罪

guilty, to feel nèijiù 内疚

H

hair tóufa 头发

half yíbàn 一半

hall lǐtáng 礼堂

hand shǒu 手

hand out fēnfā 分发

hand over yíjiāo 移交

handicap zhàng'ài 障碍

handicraft shǒugōngyìpǐn
手工艺品

handle bǎshǒu 把手

handle, to chùlǐ 处理

handsome yīngjùn 英俊

hang, to guà 挂

happen, occur fāshēng 发生

happened, what happened?
fāshēng shénme shì?
发生什么事?

happening, incident shìjiàn
事件

happy kāixīn/gāoxìng
开心 / 高兴

happy birthday! shēngrì
kuàilè! 生日快乐!

happy new year! xīnnián hǎo
新年好

harbor gǎngkǒu 港口

hard disk/drive (computer)
yìngpán 硬盘

hardly jiǎnzhí bù 简直不

hardworking, industrious
yònggōng/qínfèn
用功 / 勤奋

harmonious róngqià 融洽

hat màozi 帽子

hate, to hèn 恨

hatred chóuhèn 仇恨

have, own yǒu 有

H

have been somewhere qùguo
去过

have done something zuòguo
做过

have to, must děi 得

he, him tā 他

head tóu 头

head for, toward cháo ...
qiánjìn 朝 ... 前进

headache tóuténg/tóutòng
头疼 / 头痛

headdress tóujīn 头巾

healthy jiànkāng 健康

hear, to tīngjiàn 听见

heart xīnzàng 心脏

heat, to jiārè 加热

heavy zhòng 重

height gāodù 高度

height (body) shēn'gāo
身高

hello, hi Nǐ hǎo 你好

hello! (on phone) wèi 喂

help! Jiùmìng a! 救命啊 !

help, to bāngzhù/bāngmáng
帮助 / 帮忙

her, hers tāde 她的

here zhèbiān/zhèlǐ/zhèr
这边 / 这里 / 这儿

hidden yǐncáng 隐藏

hide, to cángqǐlái 藏起来

high gāo 高

hill qiū/xiǎoshān 丘 / 小山

hinder, to zǔ'ài 阻碍

hindrance zhàng'ài 障碍

hire, to zū 租

his tāde 他的

history lìshǐ 历史

hit, strike dǎ 打

hobby àihào 爱好

hold, to (event) jǔbài 举办

hold, to (grasp) zhuāzhe
抓着

hold back kòngzhì 控制

hole dòng 洞

holiday (festival) jiérì 节日

holiday (vacation) jiàrì 假日

holy shénshèng 神圣

home, house jiā 家

honest chéngshí de 诚实的

honey fēngmì 蜂蜜

Hong Kong Xiānggǎng
香港

hope, to xīwàng 希望

hopefully yǒu xīwàng de
有希望地

horse mǎ 马

hospital yīyuàn 医院

host zhǔrén 主人

hot (spicy) là 辣

hot (temperature) rè 热

hot spring wēnquán 温泉

hotel lǚguǎn/bīn'guǎn
旅馆 / 宾馆

hour xiǎoshí/zhōngtóu
小时 / 钟头

house fángzi 房子

how? zěnme 怎么

how are you? nǐ hǎo ma?
你好吗 ?

how far? Duō yuǎn? 多远 ?

how long? Duō cháng?
多长 ?

how many? Duōshao?/Jǐ ge?
多少 / 几个 ?

how much? Duōshao qián?
多少钱 ?

how old? Duō dà niánjì/
suìshù? 多大年纪 / 岁数 ?

however dànshì 但是

huge jùdàde 巨大的

human (feelings) rénqíngwèi
人情味

humid cháoshī 潮湿

humorous yōumòde 幽默的

hundred bǎi 百

hundred million yì/wànwàn
亿 / 万万

hundred thousand shíwàn
十万

hungry è 饿

hurry up! gǎnkuài! 赶快 !

hurt (injured) shòushāng 受伤

hurt, to (cause pain) shānghài
伤害

husband zhàngfu 丈夫

hut, shack péngwū 棚屋

I

I, me wǒ 我
ice bīng 冰
ice cream bīngjīlíng/bīngqílín
冰激凌／冰淇淋
idea zhǔyi 主意
identical tóngyīde/tóngyàng
同一的／同样
if rúguǒ/yàoshi 如果／要是
ignore, to búgù/hūshì
不顾／忽视
ignorant wúzhī 无知
ill, sick yǒubìngde 有病的
illegal fēifǎ 非法
illness bìng 病
imagine, to xiǎngxiàng 想象
immediately lìkè 立刻
impolite bú kèqi/wúlǐ
不客气／无礼
import, to import jìnkǒu 进口
importance zhòngyào 重要
important zhòngyàode 重要的
impossible bù kěnéng 不可能
impression, to make an
gěi rén shēnkè yìnxiàng
给人深刻印象
impressive gěi rén shēnkè
yìnxiàng de 给人深刻印象的
in (time, years) zài 在
in, at (space) zài ... lǐ 在... 里
in addition cǐwài 此外
incense xiāng 香
incident shìjiàn 事件
included, including bāokuò
包括
increase, to increase zēngjiā
增加
indeed! shìde 是的
indigenous (in general)
tǔzhùde 土著的
indigenous (people) tǔzhùrén
土著人
India Yìndù 印度
Indian (in general) Yìndùde
印度的
Indian (language) Yìndùyǔ
印度语

Indian (people) Yìndùrén
印度人
Indonesia Yìnní/Yìndùníxīyà
印尼／印度尼西亚
Indonesian (in general)
Yìnníde 印尼的
Indonesian (language)
Yìnníyǔ 印尼语
Indonesian (people)
Yìnnírén 印尼人
inexpensive piányi 便宜
influence, to influence
yǐngxiǎng 影响
inform, to tōngzhī 通知
information xìnxī 信息
information desk xúnwènchù
询问处
inhabitant jūmín 居民
inject, to zhùrù 注入
injection dǎzhēn 打针
injured shòushāng 受伤
injury shānghài 伤害
in order that, so that yǐzhì
以致
ink mòshuǐ 墨水
insane fēngkuángde
疯狂的
insect chóngzi 虫子
inside lǐmiàn 里面
inside of zài ... lǐ 在... 里
inspect, to jiǎnchá 检查
instead of dàitì 代替
instruct, tell to do something
zhǐshì 指示
insult wūrǔ 侮辱
insult someone, to wūrǔ
mǒurén 侮辱某人
insurance bǎoxiǎn 保险
intend, to dǎsuàn 打算
intended for wèi ... nǐdìng de
为 ... 拟定的
intention yìtú 意图
interest (bank) lìxī 利息
interested in gǎn xìngqù
感兴趣
interesting yǒuqù 有趣
international guójì 国际
Internet Yīngtèwǎng 英特网

interpreter fānyì/kǒuyìyuán 翻译／口译员
intersection shízìlùkǒu 十字路口
into dào ... lǐ 到...里
introduce oneself, to zìwǒ jièshào 自我介绍
introduce someone, to jièshào 介绍
invent, to fāmíng 发明
invitation, to invite yāoqǐng 邀请
invoice fāpiào 发票
involve, to shèjí 涉及
involved shèjídào 涉及到
Ireland Ài'ěrlán 爱尔兰
Irish (in general) Ài'ěrlánde 爱尔兰的
Irish (people) Ài'ěrlánrén 爱尔兰人
iron (for clothing) yùndǒu 熨斗
iron (metal) tiě 铁
iron, to (clothing) yùn yīfu 熨衣服
Islam Yīsīlánjiào 伊斯兰教
island dǎo 岛
Italian (in general) Yìdàlìde 意大利的
Italian (language) Yìdàlìyǔ 意大利语
Italian (people) Yìdàlìrén 意大利人
Italy Yìdàlì 意大利
item, individual thing wùpǐn/shìxiàng/tiáokuǎn 物品／事项／条款
ivory xiàngyá 象牙

J

jacket wàitào 外套
jail jiānyù 监狱
jam guǒjiàng 果酱
January Yīyuè 一月
Japan Rìběn 日本
Japanese (in general) Rìběnde 日本的

Japanese (language) Rìwén/Rìyǔ 日文／日语
Japanese (people) Rìběnrén 日本人
jaw, (lower) xià'è 下颚
jaw, (upper) shàng'è 上颚
jealous dùjì/jìdu 妒忌／忌妒
jewelry zhūbǎo/shǒushì 珠宝／首饰
job gōngzuò 工作
join, go along cānjiā 参加
join together, to liánjiēqǐlái 连接起来
joke xiàohuà 笑话
journalist jìzhě 记者
journey lùtú 路途
jug, pitcher hú 壶
juice guǒzhī 果汁
July Qīyuè 七月
jump, to tiào 跳
June Liùyuè 六月
jungle cónglín 丛林
just, fair gōngpíng 公平
just now gāngcái 刚才
just, only zhǐ 只

K

keep, to liú 留
key (computer) jiàn 键
key (to room) yàoshi 钥匙
keyboard (of computer) jiànpán 键盘
kidney shèn 肾
kidney beans dāodòu 刀豆
kill, murder shā 杀
kilogram gōngjīn 公斤
kilometer gōnglǐ 公里
kind, good (of persons) réncí 仁慈
kind, type zhǒnglèi 种类
king guówáng 国王
kiss wěn 吻
kiss, to qīnzuǐ 亲嘴
kitchen chúfáng 厨房
kiwi fruit míhóutáo 猕猴桃
knee xīgài 膝盖

ENGLISH—CHINESE

K

knife dāozi 刀子
knock, to qiāomén 敲门
know, be acquainted with
   rènshi 认识
know, be informed zhīdao
   知道
knowledge zhīshi 知识
Korea, North Cháoxiǎn 朝鲜
Korea, South Hánguó 韩国
Korean (in general)
   Hánguóde/Cháoxiǎnde
   韩国的／朝鲜的
Korean (language) Hánwén/
   Hányǔ/Cháoxiǎnyǔ
   韩文／韩语／朝鲜语
Korean (North) Cháoxiǎnrén
   朝鲜人
Korean (South) Hánguórén
   韩国人

L

lacking quēshǎo/bùzú
   缺少／不足
ladder tīzi 梯子
ladle, dipper chángbǐngsháo
   长柄勺
lady nǚshì 女士
lake hú 湖
lamb, mutton yángròu 羊肉
lamp dēng 灯
land dì 地
land, to (plane) zhuólù 着陆
lane (alley) xiàng 巷
lane (of a highway) chēdào
   车道
language yǔyán 语言
Laos Lǎowō/Liáoguó
   老挝／寮国
Laotian (in general) Lǎowōde/
   Liáoguóde 老挝的／寮国的
Laotian (people) Lǎowōrén/
   Liáoguórén 老挝人／寮国人
large dà 大
last (endure) chíxù 持续
last (final) zuìhòu 最后
last night zuówǎn 昨晚

last week shàng xīngqī
   上星期
last year qùnián 去年
late chídào 迟到
late at night shēnyè 深夜
later guò yīhuǐr 过一会儿
laugh, to xiào 笑
laugh at, to qǔxiào 取笑
laws, legislation fǎlǜ 法律
lawyer lǜshī 律师
lay the table bǎi zhuōzi 摆桌子
layer céng 层
lazy lǎnduò 懒惰
lead (to be a leader) lǐngdǎo
   领导
lead (tour guide) dǎoyóu 导游
leaded petrol hánqiān qìyóu
   含铅汽油
leader lǐngdǎorén 领导人
leaf yèzi 叶子
leak, to lòushuǐ 漏水
learn, to xué/xuéxí 学／学习
least (smallest amount)
   zuìshǎo 最少
least: at least zhìshǎo 至少
leather pígé 皮革
leave (train/bus) kāichē 开车
leave, depart líkāi 离开
leave behind by accident lāxià
   拉下
leave behind for safekeeping
   liúcún 留存
leave behind on purpose
   liúxià 留下
lecture jiǎngzuò 讲座
lecturer (at university) jiǎngshī
   讲师
left, remaining shèngxiàde
   剩下的
left-hand side zuǒbiān 左边
leg tuǐ 腿
legal héfǎ 合法
legend chuánshuō 传说
lemon, citrus níngméng 柠檬
lemongrass xiāngmáo 香茅
lend, to jiè 借
length cháng/chángdù
   长／长度

less (smaller amount)
gèngshǎode 更少的
less, minus jiǎnqù 减去
lessen, reduce jiǎnshǎo 减少
lesson kè 课
let, allow ràng 让
let's (suggestion) ... ba ... 吧
let someone know, to gàosu
告诉
letter xìn 信
level (even, flat) píng 平
level (height) gāodù 高度
level (standard) biāozhǔn 标准
library túshūguǎn 图书馆
license (for driving) jiàshǐ
zhízhào 驾驶执照
license, permit zhízhào 执照
lick, to tiǎn 舔
lid gàizi 盖子
lie, tell a falsehood shuōhuǎng/
sāhuǎng 说谎 / 撒谎
lie down, to tǎngxià 躺下
life shēnghuó/shēngmìng
生活 / 生命
lifetime yībèizi 一辈子
lift (ride in car) ràng mǒurén
dāchē 让某人搭车
lift, elevator diàntī 电梯
lift, raise tíqǐ 提起
light (bright) liàng 亮
light (lamp) dēng 灯
light (not heavy) qīng 轻
lighter dǎhuǒjī 打火机
lightning shǎndiàn 闪电
like, as hǎoxiàng 好象
like, be pleased by xǐhuan
喜欢
likewise tóngyàngde 同样的
lime, citrus suānjú 酸桔
line (mark) jièxiàn 界线
line (queue) páiduì 排队
line up, to páichéng yīxiàn
排成一线
lips zuǐchún 嘴唇
liquor, alcohol jiǔ 酒
list míngdān/mùlù
名单 / 目录
listen, to tīng 听

literature wénxué 文学
little (not much) yīdiǎnr
一点儿
little (small) xiǎo 小
live (be alive) huózhe/
shēnghuó 活着 / 生活
live (stay in a place) zhù 住
liver gān 肝
load (yī chē) huòwù
(一车) 货物
load up, to zhuānghuò 装货
located, to be wèiyú 位于
lock suǒ 锁
lock, to suǒshàng 锁上
locked suǒzhù 锁住
lodge, small hotel
xiǎo lǚguǎn/kèzhàn
小旅馆 / 客栈
lonely gūdú/jìmò 孤独 / 寂寞
long (size) cháng 长
long (time) jiǔ 久
look! nǐ kàn 你看
look, seem, appear
kànshàngqù 看上去
look after kānguǎn 看管
look at, see kàn 看
look for zhǎo 找
look like xiàng 象
look out! zhùyì 注意
look up (find in book) chá 查
loose (not in packet)
sànzhuāngde 散装的
loose (wobbly) sōngdòngde
松动的
lose, be defeated shū 输
lose, mislay diūshī 丢失
lose money, to shūqián 输钱
lost (can't find way) mílù 迷路
lost (missing) shīzōngle
失踪了
lost property shīwù
zhāolǐngchù 失物招领处
lots of xǔduō 许多
lottery cǎipiào 彩票
loud dàshēng 大声
love àiqíng 爱情
love, to ài 爱
lovely kě'ài 可爱

L

low dī 底
luck yùnqì 运气
lucky xìngyùnde 幸运的
luggage xíngli 行李
lunch, midday meal wǔfàn
午饭
lunch, to eat chī wǔfàn 吃午饭
lungs fèi 肺
luxurious háohuáde 豪华的
lychee lìzhī 荔枝

M

Macau Àomén 澳门
machine, machinery jīxiè 机械
madam (term of address)
fūren/tàitai 夫人 / 太太
magazine zázhì 杂志
mahjong májiàng 麻将
mail, post xìn 信
mail, to jì 寄
main, most important zhǔyào
主要
mainly zhǔyàode 主要的
major (important) zhòngyàode
重要的
make, to zuò/zhìzào 做 / 制造
make love zuò'ài 做爱
make up, invent
xūgòu/biānzào 虚构 / 编造
Malaysia Mǎláixīyà 马来西亚
Malaysian (in general)
Mǎláixīyàde 马来西亚的
Malaysian (people)
Mǎláixīyàrén 马来西亚人
male nánxìng 男性
man nánrén 男人
manage, succeed guǎnlǐ
管理
manager jīnglǐ 经理
Mandarin (language)
Pǔtōnghuà/Guóyǔ
普通话 / 国语
mango mángguǒ 芒果
manners lǐmào 礼貌
manufacture, to zhìzào 制造
many, much hěnduō 很多

map dìtú 地图
March Sānyuè 三月
market shìchǎng 市场
married yǐhūn 已婚
marry, get married jiéhūn 结婚
mask miànjù 面具
massage, to ànmó 按摩
mat dìxí/xiǎodiànzi
地席 / 小垫子
match, game bǐsài 比赛
matches huǒchái 火柴
material, ingredient cáiliào
材料
matter, issue shìqing 事情
mattress chuángdiàn 床垫
May Wǔyuè 五月
may kěnéng 可能
maybe yěxǔ 也许
meal cān 餐
mean (cruel) kèbóde 刻薄的
mean, to (intend) yòngyì
用意
mean, to (word) biǎoshì ... yìsi
表示 ... 意思
meaning yìsi 意思
meanwhile tóngshí 同时
measure, to liáng 量
measure up fúhé biāozhǔn
符合标准
measurements chǐcùn/dàxiǎo
尺寸 / 大小
meat ròu 肉
meatball ròuwán 肉丸
medical yīliáo 医疗
medicine yào 药
meet, to jiànmiàn 见面
meeting huìyì 会议
melon guā 瓜
member chéngyuán 成员
memories huíyì 回忆
mend, to xiūbǔ 修补
menstruate, to lái yuèjīng
来月经
mention, to tídào 提到
menu càidān 菜单
merely jǐnjǐn 仅仅
mess, in a luàn-qī bā-zāo
乱七八糟

M

message liúyán/biàntiáo
留言／便条

metal jīnshǔ 金属

method fāngfǎ 方法

meter (yī) mǐ/gōngchǐ
（一）米／公尺

meter (in taxi) jìchéngqì 计程器

midday zhōngwǔ 中午

middle, center zhōngjiān 中间

middle: be in the middle of
doing something
dāngzhōng 当中

midnight wǔyè 午夜

mild (not cold) wēnnuǎnde
温暖的

mild (not severe) wēnróude
温柔的

mild (not spicy) wèidànde
味淡的

milk niúnǎi 牛奶

millimeter háomǐ 毫米

million bǎiwàn 百万

mind, brain nǎozi 脑子

mind, to be displeased jièyì
介意

mineral water kuàngquánshuǐ
矿泉水

mini wēixíngde 微型的

minor (not important) cìyào de
次要的

minus jiǎn 减

minute fēn (zhōng) 分（钟）

mirror jìngzi 镜子

misfortune búxìng 不幸

Miss xiǎojie 小姐

miss, to (bus, flight) méi
gǎnshàng 没赶上

miss, to (loved one) xiǎngniàn
想念

missing (absent) quēdiàode
缺掉的

missing (lost person) shīzōngle
失踪了

mist bówù 薄雾

mistake cuòwù 错误

mistaken nòngcuò/wùjiě
弄错／误解

misunderstanding wùhuì 误会

mix, to hùnhé 混合

mixed hùnhéde 混合的

mobile phone shǒutí/yídòng
diànhuà 手提／移动电话

modern xiàndàide 现代的

modest, simple qiānxū/
pǔshíde 谦虚／朴实的

moment (in a moment)
děng yīxià 等一下

moment (instant) piànkè 片刻

Monday Xīngqīyī/Lǐbàiyī
星期一／礼拜一

money qián 钱

monitor (of computer)
xiǎnshìqì 显示器

monkey hóuzi 猴子

month yuè 月

monument jìniànbēi 纪念碑

moon yuèliang 月亮

more (comparative)
duō yīdiǎnr 多一点儿

more of (things) gèngduōde
更多的

more or less huò duō huò
shǎo 或多或少

moreover érqiě 而且

morning zǎoshang 早上

mosque Qīngzhēnsì 清真寺

mosquito wénzi 蚊子

most (superlative) zuì 最

most (the most of) zuìduō 最多

mostly dà bùfen 大部分

moth é 蛾

mother māma/mǔqin
妈妈／母亲

mother-in-law (husband's mother)
pòpo 婆婆

mother-in-law (wife's mother)
yuèmǔ 岳母

motor, engine fādòngjī 发动机

motor vehicle qìchē 汽车

motorcycle mótuōchē 摩托车

mountain shān 山

mouse (animal) xiǎolǎoshǔ
小老鼠

mouse (computer) shǔbiāo
鼠标

moustache xiǎohúzi 小胡子

M

mouth zuǐ 嘴

move, to (house) bānjiā 搬家

move from one place to another bān 搬

movement, motion dòngzuò/ xíngdòng 动作 / 行动

movie diànyǐng 电影

movie house diànyǐngyuàn 电影院

Mr xiānsheng 先生

Mrs tàitai 太太

MSG wèijīng 味精

much, many duō 多

mud ní 泥

muscle jīròu 肌肉

music yīnyuè 音乐

musical instrument yuèqì 乐器

museum bówùguǎn 博物馆

mushrooms mógu 蘑菇

Muslim Qīngzhēn/Mùsīlín/ Huíjiào 清真 / 穆斯林 / 回教

must bìxū 必须

mutton yángròu 羊肉

my, mine wǒde 我的

myth shénhuà 神话

N

nail (finger, toe) zhǐjiǎ 指甲

nail (spike) dīngzi 钉子

naked luǒtǐde 裸体的

name míngzi/xìngmíng 名字 / 姓名

narrow xiázhǎi 狭窄

nation, country guójiā 国家

national mínzúde 民族的

nationality guójí 国籍

natural zìránde 自然的

nature zìránjiè 自然界

naughty wánpíde 顽皮的

nearby fùjìn 附近

nearly jīhū 几乎

neat, orderly zhěngjiéde 整洁的

necessary bìxū 必需

neck bózi 脖子

necklace xiàngliàn 项链

necktie lǐngdài 领带

need xūyào 需要

need, to bìxū 必需

needle zhēn 针

neighbor línjū 邻居

neither liǎngzhě dōu bù 两者都不

neither ... nor jì bù ... yòu bù 既不... 又不

nephew (paternal) zhí'ér/zhízi 侄儿 / 侄子

nephew (maternal) wàishēng 外甥

nest niǎocháo 鸟巢

net wǎng 网

network guānxiwǎng/wǎngluò 关系网 / 网络

never cónglái méiyǒu 从来没有

never mind! méiguānxi 没关系

nevertheless rán'ér 然而

new xīn 新

New Zealand Xīnxīlán 新西兰

New Zealander Xīnxīlánrén 新西兰人

news xīnwén 新闻

newspaper bào 报

next (in line, sequence) xià yī ge 下一个

next to pángbiān 旁边

next week xiàxīngqī 下星期

next year míngnián 明年

nice hǎo 好

niece (paternal) zhínǚ 侄女

niece (maternal) wàishēngnǚ 外甥女

night yè 夜

nightclothes, nightdress shuìyī 睡衣

nightly měi yè de 每夜的

nine jiǔ 九

nineteen shíjiǔ 十九

ninety jiǔshí 九十

no, not (with nouns) méiyǒu 没有

no, not (with verbs and adjectives) búshì 不是

nobody xiǎorénwù 小人物

noise cáozáshēng/zàoyīn 嘈杂声／噪音

noisy cáozáde 嘈杂的

nonsense fèihuà 废话

noodles miàntiáo 面条

noon zhōngwǔ 中午

nor yěbù 也不

normal, normally zhèngchángde/tōngcháng 正常地／通常

north běibiān 北边

north-east dōngběi 东北

north-west xīběi 西北

nose bízi 鼻子

nostril bíkǒng 鼻孔

not bù 不

not able to understand (by hearing) tīngbudǒng 听不懂

not able to understand (by reading) kànbudǒng 看不懂

not only ... but also búdàn ... érqiě 不但 ... 而且

not yet hái méi 还没

note (currency) chāopiào 钞票

note (written) biàntiáo 便条

note down, to jìxiàlái 记下来

notebook bǐjìběn 笔记本

nothing méiyǒu shénme 没有什么

notice tōngzhī 通知

notice, to zhùyì 注意

novel xiǎoshuō 小说

November Shíyīyuè 十一月

now xiànzài 现在

nowadays dāngjīn 当今

nowhere nǎr dōu bú zài 哪儿都不在

nude luǒtǐde 裸体的

numb mámùde 麻木的

number hàomǎ 号码

nurse hùshi 护士

nylon nílóng 尼龙

O

o'clock diǎn (zhōng) （点）钟

obedient fúcóngde 服从的

obey, to fúcóng 服从

object, to protest fǎnduì 反对

object, thing dōngxi 东西

occasionally ǒuránde 偶然地

occupation zhíyè 职业

ocean hǎiyáng 海洋

October Shíyuè 十月

odor, bad smell chòuqì 臭气

of, from shǔyú ... de 属于 ... 的

of course dāngrán 当然

off (gone bad) huàile 坏了

off (turned off) guānle 关了

off: to turn something off guānshàng 关上

offend dézuì/chùfàn 得罪／触犯

offer, suggest jiànyì 建议

offer (supply) tígōng 提供

office bàn'gōngshì 办公室

official, formal zhèngshìde 正式的

officials (government) guānyuán 官员

often jīngcháng 经常

oil yóu 油

okay xíng 行

old (of persons) lǎo 老

old (of things) jiù 旧

olden times, in gǔ shíhou 古时候

Olympics Àolínpǐkè Yùndònghuì/Àoyùnhuì 奥林匹克运动会／奥运会

on (of dates) zài/yú 在／于

on (turned on) kāile 开了

on, at zài ... shàng 在 ... 上

on: to turn something on kāi 开

on fire zháohuǒ 着火

on foot zǒulù 走路

o

on the way kuài dào le 快到了
on the whole zhěngtǐ lái kàn 整体来看
on time zhǔnshí 准时
once yī cì 一次
one yī 一
one-way ticket dānchéngpiào 单程票
one who, the one which ... yàng de rén? ... 样的人？
onion yángcōng 洋葱
only zhǐyǒu 只有
open kāi 开
open, to dǎkāi 打开
operating system (computer) cāozuò xìtǒng 操作系统
opinion yìjiàn 意见
opponent duìshǒu 对手
opportunity jīhuì 机会
oppose, to fǎnduì 反对
opposed, in opposition duìlìde 对立的
opposite (contrary) xiāngfǎn 相反
opposite (facing) duìmiàn 对面
optional fēiqiángzhìde 非强制的
or huòzhě 或者
orange, citrus júzi 桔子
orange (color) chéngsè 橙色
order (command) mìnglìng 命令
order (placed for food) diǎncài 点菜
order (placed for goods) dìnggòu 订购
order, sequence cìxù 次序
order, to command mìnglìng 命令
order something, to yùdìng/xià dìngdān 预订 / 下订单
orderly, organized yǒu zhìxùde 有秩序地
organize, arrange ānpái 安排
origin qǐyuán 起源
original zuìchūde 最初的

originate, come from láiyuán (yú) 来源(于)
ornament zhuāngshìpǐn 装饰品
other biéde/qítā 别的 / 其他
other (alternative) lìngwài 另外
ought to yīnggāi 应该
our (excludes the one addressed) wǒmen 我们
our (includes the one addressed) zánmen 咱们
out zài ... wài 在 ... 外
outside wàimiàn 外面
outside of zài ... wàimiàn 在 ... 外面
oval (shape) tuǒyuánxíngde 椭圆形的
oven kǎolú 烤炉
over, finished wánle 完了
over: to turn over fān'guòlái 翻过来
over there nàbiān 那边
overcast, cloudy yīntiān 阴天
overcome, to kèfú 克服
overseas hǎiwài 海外
overturned dǎfān 打翻
owe, to qiàn 欠
own, on one's dúlìde 独立的
own, personal zìjǐde 自己的
own, to yōngyǒu 拥有
oyster háo 蚝

P

pack, to bāozhuāng/shōushí 包装 / 收拾
package bāoguǒ 包裹
page yè 页
paid yǐ fùkuǎn 已付款
pain, painful tòng 痛
paint yóuqī 油漆
paint, to (a painting) huàhuàr 画画儿
paint, to (house) yóuqī 油漆

painting huàr/huìhuà
画儿 / 绘画
pair of, a yī shuāng 一双
pajamas shuìyī 睡衣
palace gōngdiàn 宫殿
pan guō 锅
panorama quánjǐng 全景
panties jǐnshēn duǎnchènkù
紧身短衬裤
pants kùzi 裤子
paper zhǐ 纸
parcel bāoguǒ 包裹
pardon me? what did you say?
shénme? 什么
parents fùmǔ 父母
park gōngyuán 公园
park, to (car) tíngchē 停车
part (not whole) bùfèn 部分
part (of machine) língjiàn
零件
participate, to cānjiā 参加
particularly, especially
yóuqíshì 尤其是
partly bùfèn 部分
partner (in business) héhuǒrén
合伙人
partner (spouse) bànlǚ/huǒbàn
伴侣 / 伙伴
party (event) jùhuì 聚会
party (political) zhèngdǎng
政党
pass, go past jīngguò 经过
pass, to (exam) jígé 及格
passenger chéngkè 乘客
passport hùzhào 护照
past, former guòqùde 过去的
past: go past yuèguò 越过
pastime xiāoqiǎn 消遣
patient (calm) nàixīn 耐心
patient (doctor's) bìngrén
病人
pattern, design shìyàng 式样
patterned fǎngzàode 仿造的
pay, to fùqián 付钱
pay attention liúyì/zhùyì
留意 / 注意
payment zhīfù 支付
peace hépíng 和平

peaceful hépíngde 和平的
peach táozi 桃子
peak, summit shāndǐng/
dǐngfēng 山顶 / 顶峰
peanut huāshēngmǐ 花生米
pear lí 梨
pearl zhēnzhū 珍珠
peas wāndòu 豌豆
peel, to bāopí 剥皮
pen gāngbǐ 钢笔
pencil qiānbǐ 铅笔
penis yīnjīng 阴茎
people rén 人
pepper (black) hēi hújiāo
黑胡椒
pepper (chilli) làjiāo 辣椒
percent bǎifēn zhī ...
百分之 ...
percentage bǎifēnbǐ 百分比
performance yǎnchū 演出
perfume xiāngshuǐ 香水
perhaps yěxǔ 也许
perhaps, probably kěnéng
可能
period (end of a sentence)
jùhào 句号
period (menstrual) yuèjīngqī
月经期
period (of time) shíqī 时期
permanent yǒngjiǔde 永久的
permit xǔkězhèng 许可证
permit, to allow
yǔnxǔ/zhǔnxǔ 允许 / 准许
person rén 人
personality xìnggé 性格
perspire, to chūhàn 出汗
pet animal chǒngwù 宠物
petrol qìyóu 汽油
petrol station jiāyóuzhàn
加油站
pharmacy, drugstore yàodiàn
药店
Philippines Fēilǜbīn 菲律宾
photocopy fùyìnjiàn 复印件
photocopy, to fùyìn 复印
photograph zhàopiàn 照片
photograph, to zhàoxiàng
照相

pick, choose tiāoxuǎn 挑选

pick up, to (someone) jiē 接

pick up, lift (something) jiǎnqǐ 捡起

pickpocket páshǒu/xiǎotōu 扒手 / 小偷

pickpocket, to tōu qiánbāo 偷钱包

picture huàr 画儿

piece, item jiàn/kuài 件 / 块

piece, portion, section suìpiàn 碎片

pierce, penetrate cìchuān 刺穿

pig zhū 猪

pills yàowǎn/yàopiàn 药丸 / 药片

pillow zhěntou 枕头

pin dàtóuzhēn 大头针

pineapple bōluó 菠萝

pink fěnhóngsè 粉红色

pitcher, jug dà shuǐguàn 大水罐

pity kělián 可怜

pity: what a pity! kěxī 可惜

place dìfang 地方

place, put fàng 放

plain (level ground) píngyuán 平原

plain (not fancy) pǔsù 朴素

plan jìhuà 计划

plan, to dǎsuàn 打算

plane fēijī 飞机

plant zhíwù 植物

plant, to zhòng 种

plastic sùliào 塑料

plate pánzi 盘子

play, to wánr 玩儿

play around zhuīqiú xiǎngshòu 追求享受

plead, to biànhù/kěnqiú 辩护 / 恳求

pleasant lìng rén yúkuàide 令人愉快的

please go ahead, please request for help qǐng 请

pleased gāoxìng/mǎnyì 高兴 / 满意

plug (bath) sāizi 塞子

plug (electric) chātóu 插头

plum lǐzi 李子

plus jiāshàng 加上

pocket kǒudài 口袋

point (in time) shíkè 时刻

point, dot jiānduān 尖端

point out zhǐchū 指出

poison dúyào 毒药

poisonous yǒudúde 有毒的

police gōng'ānjú/jǐngchájú 公安局 / 警察局

police officer jǐngchá 警察

polish, to cāliàng 擦亮

politics zhèngzhì 政治

polite yǒu lǐmào 有礼貌

poor (not rich) qióng 穷

popular liúxíng 流行

population rénkǒu 人口

pork zhūròu 猪肉

port hǎigǎng 海港

portion, serve yī fèn 一份

possess, to zhànyǒu 占有

possessions suǒyǒu 所有

possible kěnéng 可能

possibly kěnéngde 可能的

post, column zhù 柱

post, mail jì 寄

post office yóujú 邮局

postcard míngxìnpiàn 明信片

postpone, to yánqī 延期

postponed, delayed tuīchí 推迟

pot hú 壶

poultry jiāqín 家禽

pour, to dào 倒

power lìliang 力量

powerful qiángdàde 强大的

practice, to practice liànxí 练习

praise zànyáng 赞扬

praise, to biǎoyáng 表扬

prawn xiā 虾

prayer, to pray qídǎo 祈祷

prefer, to xǐ'ài 喜爱

pregnant huáiyùn 怀孕

prepare, make ready zhǔnbèi 准备

prepared, ready zhǔnbèihǎole
准备好了
prescription yàofāng 药方
present (here) xiànzài 现在
present (gift) lǐwù 礼物
present, to jiǎngyǎn 讲演
presently, nowadays xiànzài
现在
present moment, at the
mùqiánde 目前的
president zǒngtǒng 总统
press, journalism xīnwénjiè
新闻界
press, to yā 压
pressure yālì 压力
pretend, to jiǎzhuāng 假装
pretty (of places, things)
měilì/měihǎo 美丽 / 美好
pretty (of women)
qiào/piàoliang 俏 / 漂亮
pretty, very xiāngdāng 相当
prevent, to zǔzhǐ 阻止
price jiàqián 价钱
pride zìháo/jiāo'ào
自豪 / 骄傲
priest shénfù/mùshī
神父 / 牧师
prime minister zǒnglǐ 总理
print, to (from computer)
dǎyìn 打印
prison jiānyù 监狱
private sīrénde 私人的
probably dàgài 大概
problem wèntí 问题
produce, to shēngchǎn 生产
profession zhíyè 职业
profit lìrùn 利润
program, schedule jiémù 节目
promise, to dāyìng 答应
pronounce, to fāyīn 发音
proof zhèngjù 证据
property cáichǎn 财产
protest, to kàngyì 抗议
proud jiāo'ào 骄傲
prove, to zhèngmíng 证明
public gōnggòng 公共
publish, to chūbǎn 出版
pull, to lā 拉

pump bèng 泵
punctual zhǔnshí 准时
pupil xuésheng 学生
pure chúnde 纯的
purple zǐsè 紫色
purpose mùdì 目的
purse (for money) qiánbāo
钱包
pursue zhuīqiú 追求
push, to tuī 推
put, place fàng 放
put off, delay tuīchí 推迟
put on (clothes) chuān 穿
puzzled shòu míhuò 受迷惑
pyjamas shuìyī 睡衣

Q

qualification zīgé 资格
quarter sìfēnzhīyī 四分之一
queen nǔwáng 女王
question wèntí 问题
queue, to line up páiduì 排队
quick kuài 快
quickly hěnkuàide 很快地
quiet ānjìng 安静
quite (fairly) xiāngdāng 相当
quite (very) díquè 的确

R

radio shōuyīnjī 收音机
rail: by rail zuò huǒchē
坐火车
railroad, railway tiělù 铁路
rain yǔ 雨
rain, to xiàyǔ 下雨
raise, lift tígāo 提高
raise, to (children) fǔyǎng
抚养
RAM (computer) nèicún 内存
rank, station in life dìwèi 地位
ranking jíbié 级别
rare (scarce) xīyǒude 稀有的
rare (uncooked) bànshúde
半熟的

R

rarely, seldom nándé/ǒu'ěr
难得 / 偶尔

rat hàozi/lǎoshǔ 耗子 / 老鼠

rate, tariff jiàgé 价格

rate of exchange duìhuànlǜ
兑换率

rather, fairly bǐjiào 比较

rather than níngkě 宁可

raw, uncooked, rare shēngde
生的

reach, get to dádào 达到

react to qǐ fǎnyìng 起反应

reaction, response fǎnyìng
反应

read, to kànshū 看书

ready zhǔnbèihǎole 准备好了

ready, to get zhǔnbèi 准备

ready, to make zhǔnbèihǎo
准备好

realize, be aware of yìshídào
意识到

really (in fact) shíjì 实际

really (very) fēicháng 非常

really? zhēnde ma? 真的吗？

rear, tail hòumiàn 后面

reason yuányīn/qínglǐ
原因 / 情理

reasonable (price) gōngdào
公道

reasonable (sensible)
héqínghélǐde 合情合理的

receipt shōujù 收据

receive, to shōudào 收到

recipe shípǔ 食谱

recognize, to rènde 认得

recommend, to tuījiàn 推荐

recover (cured) kāngfú 康复

rectangle chángfāngxíng
长方形

red hóngsè 红色

reduce, to jiàngjià 降价

reduction jiǎnshǎo 减少

reflect, to fǎnyìng 反映

refrigerator bīngxiāng 冰箱

refusal, to refuse jùjué 拒绝

regarding yǒuguān 有关

region dìqū 地区

register, to guàhào 挂号

registered post guàhàoxìn
挂号信

regret, to yíhàn 遗憾

regrettably lìng rén yíhànde
令人遗憾的

regular, normal dìngqī 定期

relatives, family qīnqi 亲戚

relax, to fàngsōng 放松

release, to shìfàng 释放

religion zōngjiào 宗教

remainder, leftover shèngxiàde
剩下的

remains (historical) gǔjì 古迹

remember, to jìde 记得

remind, to tíxǐng 提醒

rent, to zū 租

repair, to xiūlǐ 修理

repeat, to chóngfù 重复

replace, to dàitì 代替

reply, response dáfù 答复

reply, to (in speech) huídá 回答

reply, to (in writing) fùxìn/dáfù
复信 / 答复

report bàogào 报告

report, to huìbào 汇报

reporter jìzhě 记者

request, to (formally) yāoqiú
要求

request, to (informally) qǐngqiú
请求

rescue, to qiǎngjiù 抢救

research yánjiū 研究

research, to diàochá/yánjiū
调查 / 研究

resemble xiāngxiàng 相像

reservation bǎoliú 保留

reserve (for animals) bǎoliúdì
保留的

reserve, to (ask for in advance)
yùdìng 预订

resident, inhabitant jūmín 居民

resolve, to (a problem) jiějué
解决

respect zūnzhòng 尊重

respect, to zūnjìng 尊敬

respond, react fǎnyìng 反应

response, reaction dáfù 答复

responsibility zérèn 责任

responsible, to be fùzé 负责

rest, remainder shèngyúde 剩余的

rest, to relax xiūxi 休息

restaurant fànguǎn 饭馆

restrain, to yìzhì 抑制

restroom xǐshǒujiān 洗手间

result jiéguǒ/xiàoguǒ 结果 / 效果

resulting from, as a result jiéguǒ 结果

resume huīfú 恢复

retired tuìxiū 退休

return, go back huíqù 回去

return, give back guīhuán 归还

return home, to huíjiā 回家

return ticket láihuípiào 来回票

reveal, to (make known) jiēshì 揭示

reveal, to (make visible) zhǎnxiàn 展现

reverse, to back up shǐ dǎotuì 使倒退

reversed, backwards fǎnxiàngde 反向的

ribbon sīdài 丝带

rice (cooked) mǐfàn 米饭

rice (plant) dàozi 稻子

rice (uncooked grains) dàmǐ 大米

rice fields dàotián 稻田

rich fùyùde 富裕的

rid: get rid of jiěchú/bǎituō 解除 / 摆脱

ride (in car) zuòchē 坐车

ride, to (bicycle) qí zìxíngchē 骑自行车

ride, to (horse) qímǎ 骑马

ride, to (motorcycle) qí mótuōchē 骑摩托车

ride, to (transport) chéngchē 乘车

right, correct zhèngquè 正确

right-hand side yòubiān 右边

right now lìkè/mǎshàng 立刻 / 马上

rights quánlì 权利

ring (jewelry) jièzhǐ 戒指

ring, to (bell) ànlíng 按铃

ring, to (on the telephone) dǎ diànhuà 打电话

rip open, to sīkāi 撕开

ripe shúde/shóude 熟的

rise, ascend shàngshēng 上升

rise, increase zēngjiā 增加

rival duìshǒu 对手

river hé 河

road lù 路

roast, grill kǎo 烤

roasted, grilled, toasted hōngkǎo 烘烤

rock shítou 石头

role juésè 角色

roof wūdǐng 屋顶

room (in hotel) fángjiān 房间

room (in house) wū 屋

room, space kōngjiān 空间

root (of plant) gēn 根

rope shéngzi 绳子

rotten fǔlànde 腐烂的

rough (not gentle) cūlǔde 粗鲁的

roughly, approximately cūlüède 粗略的

round (shape) yuánxíngde 圆形的

round, around huánrào 环绕

rubber (eraser) xiàngpícā 橡皮擦

rubber (material) xiàngjiāo 橡胶

rude wúlǐde 无礼的

rules guījù 规矩

run, to pǎo 跑

run away táopǎo 逃跑

S

sacred shénshèngde 神圣的

sacrifice jìpǐn 祭品

sacrifice, to xīshēng 牺牲

sad nánguò 难过

safe ānquán 安全

sail, to hángxíng/kāichuán 航行 / 开船

S

salary gōngzī 工资

sale (reduced prices) dà jiànmài 大贱卖

sale, for chūshòu 出售

sales assistant shòuhuòyuán 售货员

salt yán 盐

salty xián 咸

same yīyàng 一样

sample yàngběn 样本

sand shāzi 沙子

sandals liángxié 凉鞋

satisfied mǎnyìde 满意的

satisfy, to mǎnzú 满足

Saturday Xīngqīliù/Lǐbàiliù 星期六

sauce tiáowèizhī 调味汁

sauce (chilli) làjiāojiàng 辣椒酱

save, keep cún 存

say, to shuō 说

say hello dài wènhǎo 代问好

say goodbye dàobié 道别

say sorry dàoqiàn 道歉

say thank you dàoxiè 道谢

scales chèng/tiānpíng 秤 / 天平

scarce bùzúde, quēfáde 不足的 / 缺乏的

scared hàipà 害怕

scenery zìrán fēngjǐng 自然风景

schedule shíkèbiǎo/ rìchéngbiǎo 时刻表 / 日程表

school xuéxiào 学校

schoolchild zhōng/ xiǎoxuéshēng 中 / 小学生

science kēxué 科学

scissors jiǎndāo 剪刀

Scotland Sūgélán 苏格兰

Scottish (in general) Sūgélánde 苏格兰的

Scottish, Scots Sūgélánrén 苏格兰人

screen (of computer) píngmù 屏幕

screwdriver qǐzi/luósīdāo 起子 / 螺丝刀

scrub, to cāxǐ 擦洗

sculpture, to sculpt diāosù 雕塑

sea hǎi 海

seafood hǎixiān 海鲜

search for, to xúnzhǎo 寻找

season jìjié 季节

seat zuòwèi 座位

second (in sequence) dì'èr 第二

second (instant) miǎo 秒

secret mìmì 秘密

secret, to keep a bǎomì 保密

secretary mìshū 秘书

secure, safe ānquán 安全

see, to kànjiàn 看见

seed zhǒngzi 种子

seek, to zhǎo/zhuīqiú 找 / 追求

seem, to sìhū 似乎

see you later! huítóu jiàn 回头见

seldom hěnshǎo 很少

select, to tiāoxuǎn 挑选

self zìjǐ 自己

self-respect/self-esteem zìzūn 自尊

sell, to mài 卖

send, to sòng 送

sensible héqínglǐde/míngzhì 合情理的 / 明智

sentence jùzi 句子

separate fēnlíde 分离的

separate, to fēnkāi 分开

September Jiǔyuè 九月

sequence, order cìxù 次序

serious (not funny) yánsù 严肃

serious (severe) yánzhòng 严重

servant yòngrén 佣人

serve, to wèi ... fúwù 为 ... 服务

service fúwù 服务

sesame oil máyóu 麻油

sesame seeds zhīmá 芝麻

set tào 套

seven qī 七

seventeen shíqī 十七

seventy qīshí 七十
several jǐ 几
severe yánlì 严厉
sew, to féng 缝
sex, gender xìngbié 性别
sex, sexual activity xìng xíngwéi 性行为
shack péngliáo 棚寮
shade yīnliángchù 阴凉处
shadow yǐngzi 影子
shadow play píyǐngxì 皮影戏
shake, to yáo 摇
shake something, to yáohuǎng 摇晃
shall, will jiāngyào 将要
shallow qiǎn 浅
shame, disgrace xiūchǐ 羞耻
shame: what a shame! zhēn diūliǎn! 真丢脸
shampoo xǐfàjì 洗发剂
Shanghai Shànghǎi 上海
shape xíngzhuàng 形状
shape, to form xíngchéng 形成
shark shāyú 鲨鱼
sharp jiānruì 尖锐
shave, to guā húzi 刮胡子
she, her tā 她
sheet (for bed) chuángdān 床单
sheet (of paper) zhǐzhāng 纸张
sheep yáng 羊
Shinto Shéndào 神道
shiny fāliàng 发亮
ship chuán 船
shirt chènshān 衬衫
shit shǐ 屎
shiver, to fādǒu 发抖
shoes xié 鞋
shoot, to (with a gun) kāiqiāng 开枪
shop, go shopping gòuwù/mǎi dōngxi 购物 / 买东西
shop, store shāngdiàn 商店
shopkeeper diànzhǔ 店主
short (concise) duǎn 短
short (not tall) ǎi 矮

short time, a moment duǎnzàn 短暂
shorts (short trousers) duǎnkù 短裤
shorts (underpants) duǎnnèikù/hànkù 短内裤 / 汗裤
shoulder jiānbǎng 肩膀
shout, to hūhǎn 呼喊
show (live performance) biǎoyǎn 表演
show, to gěi ... kàn 给 ... 看
shower (for washing) línyù 淋浴
shower (of rain) zhènyǔ 阵雨
shower, to take a xǐ ge línyù 洗个淋浴
shrimp, prawn xiǎoxiā 小虾
shut guānbì 关闭
shut, to guānshàng 关上
sibling xiōngdìjiěmèi 兄弟姐妹
sick, ill bìngle 病了
sick to be (vomit) ǒutù 呕吐
side pángbiān 旁边
sightseeing guān'guāng 观光
sign, road lùbiāo 路标
sign, symbol biāojì 标记
sign, to qiānmíng 签名
signature qiānmíng 签名
signboard zhāopái 招牌
silent chénmòde 沉默的
silk sīchóu 丝绸
silver yín 银
similar xiāngsìde 相似的
simple (easy) róngyì 容易
simple (uncomplicated) jiǎndān 简单
since zìcóng 自从
sing, to chànggē 唱歌
Singapore Xīnjiāpō 新加坡
Singaporean (in general) Xīnjiāpōde 新加坡的
Singaporean (people) Xīnjiāpōrén 新加坡人
single (not married) dānshēn 单身
single (only one) dānyī 单一

S

sir (term of address) xiānsheng 先生

sister (older) jiějie 姐姐

sister (younger) mèimei 妹妹

sister-in-law (wife of husband's older brother) sǎozi 嫂子

sister-in-law (wife of husband's younger brother) dìxí/dìmèi 弟媳 / 弟妹

sister-in-law (wife of one's older/younger brother) jiùsǎo 舅嫂

sister-in-law (wife's older sister) yíjiě 姨姐

sister-in-law (wife's sister) yízi 姨子

sister-in-law (wife's younger sister) yímèi 姨妹

sit down, to zuòxiàlái 坐下来

situated, to be wèiyú 位于

situation, how things are qíngkuàng 情况

six liù 六

sixteen shíliù 十六

sixty liùshí 六十

size dàxiǎo 大小

skewer chuànròuqiān 串肉扦

skillful shúliànde 熟练的

skin pífū 皮肤

skirt qúnzi 裙子

sky tiānkōng 天空

sleep, to shuìjiào 睡觉

sleepy kùn 困

slender miáotiáode 苗条的

slight shǎoxǔ/xiēwēi 少许 / 些微

slightly shāowēi 稍微

slim xìchángde 细长的

slippers tuōxié 拖鞋

slope shānpō 山坡

slow màn 慢

slowly mànmānde 慢慢的

small xiǎo 小

smart cōngmíng 聪明

smell, bad odor chòuwèi 臭味

smell, to wén 闻

smile, to xiào 笑

smoke yān 烟

smoke, to (tobacco) chōuyān 抽烟

smooth (of surfaces) pínghuáde 平滑的

smooth (unproblematic) shùnlì 顺利

smuggle, to (illegal goods) zǒuzī 走私

snake shé 蛇

sneeze pēntì 喷嚏

sneeze, to dǎ pēntì 打喷嚏

snow xuě 雪

snow, to xiàxuě 下雪

snowpeas hélándòu 荷兰豆

so (degree) zhème/nàme 这么 / 那么

so, therefore suǒyǐ 所以

so that yǐzhì 以致

soak, to jìn/jìnpào 浸 / 浸泡

soap féizào 肥皂

soccer zúqiú 足球

socket (electric) chāzuò 插座

socks wàzi 袜子

sofa, couch shāfā 沙发

soft ruǎn 软

soft drink qìshuǐ 汽水

software (computer) ruǎnjiàn 软件

sold màidiào 卖掉

sold out màiwán 卖完

soldier shìbīng /士兵

sole, only zhǐshì/wéiyī 只是 / 唯一

solid gùtǐde 固体的

solve, to (a problem) jiějué 解决

some yīxiē/jǐge 一些 / 几个

somebody, someone yǒurén 有人

something shénme 什么

sometimes yǒushí 有时

somewhere shénme dìfang/ mǒuchù 什么地方/ 某处

son érzi 儿子

son-in-law nǚxu 女婿

song gē 歌

soon bùjiǔ 不久

sore, painful tòng/suāntòng
痛／酸痛
sorrow bēi'āi 悲哀
sorry, to feel regretful hòuhuǐ
后悔
sorry! duìbuqǐ/bàoqiàn
对不起／抱歉
sort, type zhǒnglèi 种类
sort out, deal with jiějué 解决
sound, noise shēngyīn 声音
soup (clear) qīngtāng 清汤
soup (spicy stew)
tāng/chóutāng 汤／稠汤
sour suān 酸
source chūchù/láiyuán
出处／来源
south nánbiān 南边
south-east dōngnán 东南
south-west xī'nán 西南
souvenir jìniànpǐn 纪念品
soy sauce (salty) xián
jiàngyóu 咸酱油
soy sauce (sweet) tián
jiàngyóu 甜酱油
space kōngjiān/dìfang
空间／地方
spacious kuānchang 宽敞
speak, to jiǎng/shuō 讲／说
special tèbié 特别
spectacles yǎnjìng 眼镜
speech jiǎnghuà 讲话
speech, to make a yǎnjiǎng
演讲
speed sùdù 速度
spell, to yòng zìmǔ pīnxiě
用字母拼写
spend, to huāqián 花钱
spices xiāngliào 香料
spicy jiā xiāngliào de
加香料的
spinach bōcài 菠菜
spine jíliánggǔ 脊梁骨
spiral luóxuánxíngde
螺旋形的
spirits, hard liquor lièjiǔ
烈酒
spoiled (of children)
chǒnghuàide 宠坏的

spoiled (of food) biànwèide
变味的
spoon sháozi 勺子
sponge hǎimián 海面
sports yùndòng 运动
spotted (pattern) yǒu
bāndiǎnde 有斑点的
spray pēnwùqì 喷雾器
spring (metal part) tánhuáng
弹簧
spring (of water)
kuàngquánshuǐ 矿泉水
spring (season) chūntiān 春天
spouse pèi'ǒu 配偶
square (shape) zhèngfāngxíng
正方形
square, town square
guǎngchǎng 广场
squid yóuyú 鱿鱼
staff gōngzuò rényuán
工作人员
stain wūdiǎn 污点
stairs lóutī 楼梯
stall (of vendor) tānzi 摊子
stall, to (car) xīhuǒ 熄火
stamp (ink) gàizhāng 盖章
stamp (postage) yóupiào 邮票
stand, to zhàn 站
stand up, to miànduì 面对
star xīngxīng 星星
start, beginning kāishǐ 开始
start, to (machine) qǐdòng
起动
stationery wénjù 文具
statue diāoxiàng 雕像
stay, remain liúxià 留下
stay overnight, to liúsù/guòyè
留宿／过夜
steal, to tōu 偷
steam zhēngqì 蒸汽
steamed zhēngde 蒸的
steel gāngtiě 钢铁
steer, to jiàshǐ 驾驶
step bù 步
steps, stairs táijiē 台阶
stick, pole gùn 棍
stick out, to tūchū 突出
stick to, to jiānchí 坚持

S

sticky zhànxìngde 粘性的
sticky rice nuòmǐ 糯米
stiff yìngde 硬的
still, even now réngrán 仍然
still, quiet píngjìngde 平静的
stingy lìnsè 吝啬
stink, to fāchòu 发臭
stomach, belly dùzi 肚子
stone shítou 石头
stool dèngzi 凳子
stop (bus, train) zhàn 站
stop, to cease tíng 停
stop, to halt tíngzhǐ 停止
stop by, to pay a visit shùnlù
　bàifǎng 顺路拜访
stop it! bié zài zhèyàng
　别再这样
store, shop shāngdiàn 商店
store, to chǔzáng 储藏
storm fēngbào 风暴
story (of a building) céng/lóu
　层 / 楼
story (tale) gùshi 故事
stout zhuàngshí 壮实
stove, cooker lúzi 炉子
straight (not crooked) zhíde
　直的
straight ahead yīzhí zǒu
　一直走
strait hǎixiá 海峡
strange qíguài 奇怪
stranger mòshēngrén 陌生人
street jiē 街
strength lìliang 力量
strict yán'gé 严格
strike, hit dǎjī 打击
strike, to go on bàgōng 罢工
string shéngzi 绳子
striped yǒutiáowénde
　有条纹的
strong qiángzhuàng 强壮
stubborn, determined
　wángùde 顽固的
stuck, won't move xiànzhù
　陷住
student xuésheng 学生
study, learn xué/xuéxí
　学 / 学习

stupid bèn/chǔn 笨 / 蠢
style fēnggé 风格
succeed, to jìchéng/
　chénggōng 继承 / 成功
success chénggōng 成功
such zhèyàng/rúcǐ
　这样 / 如此
such as, for example lìrú 例如
suck, to xī 吸
suddenly tūrán 突然
suffer, to shòu tòngkǔ 受痛苦
suffering tòngkǔ 痛苦
sugar táng 糖
sugarcane gānzhè 甘蔗
suggestion, to suggest jiànyì
　建议
suit, business yī tào xīfú
　一套西服
suitable, fitting héshìde
　合适的
suitcase xiāngzi 箱子
summer xiàtiān, 夏天
summit, peak shāndǐng 山顶
sun tàiyáng 太阳
Sunday Xīngqī'tiān/ rì,
　Lǐbài'tiān/rì 星期天 / 日 ,
　礼拜天 / 日
sunlight yángguāng 阳光
sunny qínglǎng 晴朗
sunscreen lotion fángshàiyóu
　防晒油
sunrise rìchū 日出
sunset rìluò 日落
supermarket chāojí
　shìchǎng/chāoshì
　超级市场 / 超市
suppose, to jiǎdìng 假定
sure kěndìng/quèdìng
　肯定 / 确定
surf chōnglàng 冲浪
surfing on the Internet
　shàngwǎng qù chōnglàng
　上网去冲浪
surface biǎomiàn 表面
surface mail hǎi-lù yóujì
　海陆邮寄
surname xìng 姓
surprised jīngqí 惊奇

surprising shǐ rén jīngqí de 使人惊奇的
surroundings huánjìng 环境
survive, to huóxiàlái 活下来
suspect, to huáiyí 怀疑
suspicion yíxīn 疑心
swallow, to tūn 吞
sweat hàn 汗
sweat, to chūhàn 出汗
sweep, to sǎo 扫
sweet (taste) tián 甜
sweet, dessert tiánshí 甜食
sweet and sour tángcù/ suāntián 糖醋／酸甜
sweetcorn yùmǐ 玉米
sweets, candy tángguǒ 糖果
swim, to yóuyǒng 游泳
swimming costume yóuyǒngyī 游泳衣
swimming pool yóuyǒngchí 游泳池
swing, to yáobǎi 摇摆
switch kāiguān 开关
switch, to change zhuǎn 转
switch on, turn on kāi 开
synthetic héchéngde 合成的
system xìtǒng 系统

T

table zhuōzi 桌子
tablecloth zhuōbù 桌布
tablemat diànzi 垫子
tablets yàopiàn 药片
tail wěiba 尾巴
take, to remove názǒu 拿走
take care of, to zhàoguǎn 照管
take off (clothes) tuō 脱
talk, to tánhuà 谈话
talk about tánlùn 谈论
tall gāo 高
tame xúnfúde 驯服的
Taoism Dàojiào 道教
tape, adhesive jiāodàizhǐ 胶带纸
tape recording lùyīn 录音

taste wèidào 味道
taste, to (sample) cháng 尝
taste, to (salty, spicy) chángwèi 尝味
tasty hǎochī 好吃
taxi chūzūqìchē 出租汽车
tea chá 茶
teach, to jiāo 教
teacher jiàoshī/lǎoshī 教师／老师
team duì 队
tear, to rip sīkāi 撕开
tears yǎnlèi 眼泪
teenager qīngshàonián 青少年
teeshirt hànshān 汗衫
teeth yá 牙
telephone diànhuà 电话
telephone number diànhuà hàomǎ 电话号码
television diànshì 电视
tell, to (a story) jiǎng 讲
tell, to (let know) gàosu 告诉
temperature (body) tǐwēn 体温
temperature (heat) wēndù 温度
temple (Chinese) sìyuàn 寺院
temporary zànshí 暂时
ten shí 十
ten million qiānwàn 千万
ten thousand wàn 万
tendon jīn 筋
tennis wǎngqiú 网球
tens of, multiples of ten jǐ shí 几十
tense jǐnzhāngde 紧张的
terrible kěpà 可怕
test shìyàn 试验
test, to cèyàn 测验
testicles gāowán 睾丸
than bǐ 比
Thai (in general) Tàiguóde 泰国的
Thai (language) Tàiyǔ 泰语
Thai (people) Tàiguórén 泰国人
Thailand Tàiguó 泰国

T

thank, to gǎnxiè 感谢
thank you xièxie 谢谢
that, those nà, nàxiē 那，那些
theater (drama) jùyuàn 剧院
their, theirs tāmen de 他们的
then ránhòu 然后
there nàbiān/nàli/nàr
  那边 / 那里 / 那儿
there is, there are yǒu 有
therefore yīncǐ 因此
they, them tāmen 他们
thick (of liquids) nóng 浓
thick (of things) hòu 厚
thief zéi 贼
thigh dàtuǐ 大腿
thin (of liquids) xī 稀
thin (of persons) shòu 瘦
thing dōngxi/shìwù 东西 / 事物
think, to have an opinion
  rènwéi 认为
think, to ponder xiǎng/kǎolǜ
  想 / 考虑
third (1/3) sānfēn zhī yī
  三分之一
third (in a series) dìsān 第三
thirsty kě 渴
thirty sānshí 三十
this, these zhè, zhèxiē
  这，这些
though suīrán 虽然
thoughts xiǎngfa/sīxiǎng
  想法 / 思想
thousand qiān 千
thread xiàn 线
threaten, to kǒnghè 恐吓
three sān 三
throat hóulóng 喉咙
through, past tōngguò 通过
throw, to rēng 扔
throw away, throw out
  rēngdiào 扔掉
thunder dǎléi 打雷
Thursday Xīngqīsì/Lǐbàisì
  星期四 / 礼拜四
thus, so zhèyàng/yúshì
  这样 / 于是
ticket piào 票
tidy zhěngjié 整洁

tidy up shōushí 收拾
tie, necktie lǐngdài 领带
tie, to jì 系
tiger lǎohǔ 老虎
tight jǐn 紧
time shíjiān 时间
time: from time to time yǒushí
  有时
times (multiplying) chéng 乘
timetable shíkèbiāo 时刻表
tiny jíxiǎode 极小的
tip (end) jiānduān 尖端
tip (gratuity) xiǎofèi 小费
tired (sleepy) kùn 困
tired (worn out) lèi 累
title (of book, film) biāotí 标题
title (of person) tóuxián 头衔
to, toward (a person)
  xiàng/duì 向 / 对
to, toward (a place) wǎng/cháo
  往 / 朝
today jīntiān 今天
toe jiǎozhǐ 脚趾
tofu dòufu 豆腐
together yīqǐ 一起
toilet cèsuǒ/xǐshǒujiān
  厕所 / 洗手间
tomato xīhóngshì 西红柿
tomorrow míngtiān 明天
tongue shétou 舌头
tonight jīnwǎn 今晚
too (also) yě 也
too (excessive) tài 太
too much tài duō/guòfèn
  太多 / 过分
tool gōngjù 工具
tooth yá 牙
toothbrush yáshuā 牙刷
toothpaste yágāo 牙膏
top dǐng 顶
topic tímù 题目
torch, flashlight shǒudiàntǒng
  手电筒
total yīgòng 一共
touch, to mō/chù 摸 / 触
tourist lǚyóuzhě/yóukè
  旅游者 / 游客
toward (people/place) xiàng 向

ENGLISH—CHINESE

ENGLISH—CHINESE

towel máojīn 毛巾
tower tǎ 塔
town shìzhèn 市镇
toy wánjù 玩具
trade màoyì 贸易
trade, to exchange jiāoyì
交易
traditional chuántǒngde
传统的
traffic jiāotōng 交通
train huǒchē 火车
train station huǒchēzhàn
火车站
training xùnliàn 训练
translate, to fānyì/bǐyì
翻译 / 笔译
travel, to lǚxíng 旅行
traveler lǚyóuzhě/lǚkè
旅游者 / 旅客
tray tuōpán 托盘
treat (something special) lèshì
乐事
treat, to (behave towards)
duìdài 对待
treat, to (medically) zhìliáo 治疗
tree shù 树
triangle sānjiǎoxíng 三角形
tribe bùluò 部落
trip, journey lǚxíng/lǚchéng
旅行 / 旅程
troops bùduì 部队
trouble máfan 麻烦
troublesome fánnǎode/
máfande 烦恼的 / 麻烦的
trousers kùzi 裤子
truck kǎchē 卡车
true zhēnde 真的
truly zhēnchéngde 真诚的
trust, to xìnrèn 信任
try, to shì 试
try on (clothes) shìchuān 试穿
Tuesday Xīngqī'èr/Lǐbài'èr
星期二 / 礼拜二
turn around, to zhuǎn 转
turn off, to guānshang 关上
turn on, to kāi 开
turtle (land) wūguī 乌龟
turtle (sea) hǎiguī 海龟

TV diànshì 电视
twelve shí'èr 十二
twenty èrshí 二十
twice liǎng cì 两次
two (measure) liǎng 两
two (numeral) èr 二
type, sort zhǒnglèi 种类
type, to dǎzì 打字
typhoon táifēng 台风
typical diǎnxíngde 典型的

U

ugly nánkàn/chǒu 难看 / 丑
umbrella sǎn 伞
uncle (father's older brother)
bófù/bóbo 伯父 / 伯伯
uncle (father's younger brother)
shūfù/shūshu 叔父 / 叔叔
uncle (husband of father's
sister) gūzhàng 姑丈
uncle (husband of mother's
sister) yífu 姨夫
uncle (mother's brother)
jiùfù/jiùjiu 舅父 / 舅舅
under zài ... dǐxià 在 ... 底下
undergo, to jīngguò 经过
underpants nèikù 内裤
undershirt nèiyī 内衣
understand dǒng/míngbai
懂 / 明白
understood (by hearing)
tīngdǒng/tīngmíngbai
听懂 / 听明白
understood (by reading)
kàndǒng/kànmíngbai
看懂 / 看明白
underwear nèiyī 内衣
undressed, to get tuō yīfu
脱衣服
unemployed shīyè 失业
unfortunately yíhànde
遗憾地
unhappy bù gāoxìng 不高兴
United Kingdom Yīngguó
英国
United States Měiguó 美国

U

university dàxué 大学
unleaded petrol hánqiān qìyóu
含铅汽油
unless chúfēi 除非
unlucky dǎoméide 倒霉的
unnecessary duōyúde 多余的
unripe wèichéngshúde
未成熟的
until zhídào 直到
up, upward xiàngshàng 向上
upset, unhappy fánmèn 烦闷
upside down diāndǎo 颠倒
upstairs lóushàng 楼上
urban chéngshìde 城市的
urge, to push for cuīcù 催促
urgent jǐnjí 紧急
urinate, to xiǎobiàn/jiě
xiǎobiàn 小便／解小便
us wǒmen 我们
us (includes the one
addressed) zánmen 咱们
use, to yòng 用
used to xíguàn 习惯
useful yǒuyòngde 有用的
useless wúyòngde 无用的
usual wǎngcháng 往常
usually tōngcháng 通常
uterus zǐgōng 子宫

V

vacation jiàqī 假期
vaccination dǎ fángyìzhēn
打防疫针
vagina yīndào 阴道
vague hánhúde 含糊的
valid yǒuxiào 有效
valley shāngǔ 山谷
value (cost) jiàzhí 价值
value, good zhíde 值得
value, to zhòngshì 重视
vase huāpíng 花瓶
VCR lùxiàngjī 录象机
vegetable shūcài 蔬菜
vegetarian chīsùde 吃素的
vehicle chē 车
vertical chuízhíde 垂直的

very, extremely hěn 很
vest, undershirt bèixīn 背心
via jīngyóu 经由
video cassette lùxiàngdài
录象带
video recorder lùxiàngjī
录象机
videotape, to shèxiàng 摄像
Vietnam Yuènán 越南
Vietnamese (in general)
Yuènánde 越南的
Vietnamese (language)
Yuènányǔ 越南语
Vietnamese (people)
Yuènánrén 越南人
view, look at guānkàn 观看
view, panorama fēngjǐng
风景
village cūnzhuāng 村庄
vinegar cù 醋
visa qiānzhèng 签证
visit cānguān 参观
visit, to pay a fǎngwèn 访问
voice shēngyīn 声音
voicemail diànhuà liúyán
电话留言
volcano huǒshān 火山
vomit, to ǒutù 呕吐
vote, to tóupiào 投票

W

wages gōngzī 工资
wait for, to děng 等
waiter, waitress fúwùyuán
服务员
wake up xǐnglái 醒来
wake someone up jiàoxǐng
叫醒
Wales Wēi'ěrsī 威尔斯
walk, to zǒu 走
walking distance zǒudédào de
jùlí 走得到的距离
wall qiáng 墙
wallet qiánbāo 钱包
want, to yào 要
war zhànzhēng 战争